D1413815

DISCARDED

St. Lucie West Library
Indian River Community College
500 NW California Blvd.
Port St. Lucie, FL 34986

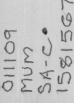

PUBLICITY

PUBLICITY

7 STEPS

TO PUBLICIZE JUST ABOUT ANYTHING

Glitterati

INCORPORATED

New York, New York

DAVID CARRIERE

First published in the United States of America in 2008 by

225 Central Park West
New York, New York 10024
www.GlitteratiIncorporated.com

Copyright © 2008 David Carriere

All rights reserved. No part of this publication may be reproduced in any form or by
any electronic or mechanical means, including information storage and retrieval
systems, without permission in writing from Glitterati Incorporated, except by a
reviewer who may quote brief passages in a review.

First edition, 2008

Design by Paul Palmer-Edwards
Grade Design Ltd, London
www.gradedesign.com

Library of Congress Cataloging-in-Publication data is available from the Publisher.

Hardcover ISBN 13: 978 0 9793384 7 2

Printed and bound in Hong Kong by Hong Kong Graphics & Printing Ltd

10 9 8 7 6 5 4 3 2 1

To my nephew, Kevin Cavanaugh:

You are a courageous teacher
in and out of the classroom,
and my respect for you is immense.

CONTENTS

INTRODUCTION

THOUGH I HAVE NEVER BEEN EMPLOYED AS A WRITER, I HAVE HAD TO EMPLOY A BIT OF WRITING OVER THE PAST TWENTY YEARS AS PART OF MY WORK AS A PUBLICIST, AND AS A RESULT OF THAT EXPERIENCE, I HAVE WANTED TO MAKE WRITING MORE OF A PRIORITY IN MY LIFE. I have often heard it said that if you want to write, then you should start by writing about something you know. I've come to know the world of publicity, so I decided to write this introduction drawing from my own experience in the field. From the start, I have attempted not only to thread examples and lessons from my own career throughout the work, but also to personalize the book with my own thumbprint, just as I urge every publicist to do when working on a campaign.

I actually wrote the bones of this book about ten years ago in the TriBeCa area of New York City as a means to decompress after I decided to leave my job at a big publishing house. Then I put a hard copy of the first draft in a file, moved to the countryside, and ignored it for a decade. Even though how to generate publicity is actually the one subject matter that I felt qualified to write something about, it was also the one subject that would position me as "that publicity guy," or some such character from central casting that I didn't want to be. Now, it's ten years later, and as I celebrate my twenty years as a publicist, I realize that while I am by no means an expert on this topic, I have some street smarts and have made a living for more than two decades by creating publicity. Frankly, for better or for worse, I have realized that I *am* "that publicity guy."

My years orchestrating publicity campaigns have pretty much been evenly split between my first ten years, when I learned the ropes from the inside at corporate jobs at both large publishing houses and small book packagers in big cities on both coasts, and the past ten years or so, which I have spent doing the same work, but for myself, and out of my home office in a rural setting. Let me assure you: I know firsthand from my own experience in all of these various scenarios, from high-pressure meetings in corporate towers to sleepy mornings spent with my laptop in hand, staring at the seasons passing from the window of my old house, that you can publicize just about anything from just about anywhere—I have done it, and you can, too.

Let me also say right from the very start that this book is a primer, and that it was written only to serve as a basic introduction to what many newcomers consider the mysterious and intimidating process of generating publicity. Each publicity campaign is unique, so this book offers an overview of the entire process, whether in the publishing industry or not. Written for the budding publicist in any industry, for individuals who simply want to better understand how to generate press attention, and for those who retain publicists yet wonder what they do, this book is informative for one and for all. Generating publicity is not about knowing some wonderful secret, or about knowing the right people, or about having good luck, as much as it is about employing a methodology and a series of steps in a thoughtful and fairly labor-intensive process.

I once received a call from a friend's father, who I hardly knew. As he had just written a book that was about to be published, he wondered if we could have a chat to discuss what he might expect from his publisher's publicity department in the months ahead. I receive this type of request fairly often, and I am usually happy to oblige as I consider such calls from friends professional courtesies, so I was happy to speak with him for more than an hour on a sunny Saturday afternoon. Because he was seeking my advice, I had assumed from the start that he was green as far as publicity went, and he seemed very low-key and shy to me over the phone as we talked away. I had no idea how to read the way the conversation was going until the very end of our call, when he curtly exclaimed, "Tell me something I don't know about publicity—I ran the marketing department of a major corporation for a number of years, and I already know everything you are telling me!" Frankly, I was stunned, and didn't realize until that moment that the best advice I could give this man who knew everything about publicity was, "Be nice, nobody likes a jerk!" The point is that this book's thesis is probably not going to offer the experienced publicist any magic bullets, but I do expect that it will offer the novice and the simply inquisitive enough insight into the process that it will serve as a solid road map and guide.

Publicity is organized in a chronological manner that will inspire the budding publicist to move with ease from the early conceptual stage of a campaign through the demanding steps of executing such a project from start to finish. I have been very fortunate throughout my career in that a few generous mentors and colleagues have taught me the ropes and helped me develop my own instincts, so I now stand on their shoulders as I share that which through the years has become my own system for creating successful publicity campaigns. Through publicizing all kinds of people, from authors to hairstylists, and all kinds of companies, from modern dance troupes to publishing houses, I consistently honed my own practical step-by-step approach toward generating publicity and can now offer the reader an easy-to-follow method that covers the nitty-gritty details as well as the comprehensive big picture in publicizing just about anything. You don't have to be experienced in this field as much as you need to be organized and confident enough, as well as dedicated and disciplined enough, to invest the energy and time to make your message stand out and seduce your target. Various individuals, with a myriad of pitches, are constantly approaching the media with floods of information and with literally and figuratively tons of content, so the key to any publicist's success lies in crafting a succinct message, casting a wide net in a timely manner, and confidently riding the publicity highway, with all its ups and downs.

Finally, for the sake of being consistent with language throughout this text, from this point forward I will address you, the reader, as a working publicist. In addition, no matter what you are publicizing, and no matter what the focus of your thoughts or campaign may be, for the sake of simplicity and consistency, I am also going to use the word "product" throughout the book when referring to the subject of your efforts. You, the reader, can alter this word in your mind every time you read it to represent your "photographer," or "client," or "restaurant," or "service," or "book," or "author," or "nonprofit," or "school," or whatever lies at the center of your campaign.

CHAPTER 1 | GETTING PREPARED

Are we there yet?

ANYONE PLANNING A LONG TREK KNOWS FROM THE START THAT PATIENCE IS REQUIRED WHILE TRAVELING THE DISTANCE, MILE BY MILE. GENERATING PUBLICITY IS ALSO A JOURNEY—ONE THAT REQUIRES PERSISTENCE AS WELL AS PROPER PLANNING, THE RIGHT EQUIPMENT, A BUDGET, A TIMELINE, AND A MAP IN ORDER TO NAVIGATE TO THE DESTINATION.

The truth is the publicity process takes an investment of time, and it requires some discipline and a dash of gumption to execute a publicity campaign. The good news, however, is that it doesn't usually require much of a budget. One might even consider mounting an entire campaign electronically, using only technology that essentially costs nothing, as long as the equipment is in place. Sure, it helps the cause if you have buckets of money to throw around, but it's not really necessary. Publicity is earned media, rather than paid media, like advertising. So, other than paying for the time of other people, and for some basics, such as office supplies and press kit contents, the financial aspect of a publicity campaign usually isn't much of a challenge. In fact, the publicity campaign is the one budget item in an entire marketing endeavor that is usually very fiscally manageable. Since that is the case, whether you are publishing a book, running for office, assisting a nonprofit, or opening a restaurant—whatever the "product" may be—you need to consider the publicity potential that exists. At the end of the day, you don't have to end up doing anything, but you should at least consider from the beginning all of the possibilities that are truly within your reach. If you decide that you are prepared to proceed, have a goal, and have envisioned a destination, then all you need to do is create a road map to get there.

There was an era not long ago when respectable ladies and gentlemen wanted their names in the newspaper only twice in their lives—once when they married and once when they died! Nowadays, all of the rules have changed—these are competitive and media-crazy times, and everyone from actors to musicians and illustrators to bakers needs to use the power of publicity like never before. You, too, must be competitive, because you are not only fighting the obvious competitors in your own particular profession for page space and airtime, but you are in a sense actually fighting everyone and everything in every category out there with a publicist attached. There are only so many working magazine editors, and they only have so many column inches to offer; there are only so many television producers, and they only control so much on-air time— they all only want what they want, and they only need what they need. On top of that, the landscape is always evolving and changing for all of those involved, so to score publicity in today's mad environment, you must be savvy enough to embrace the ever-emerging tools that technology offers, while at the same time striving to make old human connections the good-old-fashioned way.

They need you just as much as you need them

Think about it for a minute: newspapers need to fill every page of every edition every day. Radio and television producers often have hours of airtime that need to be scheduled, each and every day. Magazine editors must constantly consider, gather, and produce huge amounts of unique content that gives them the edge over their competitors. You might be asking yourself, "Why would they pay attention to me?" The answer is that they need to keep their fingers on the pulses of, be aware of, and consider the gamut of each and every option available to them. Obviously, not every person you approach will be receptive to your pitch, let alone give you the time of day, but if you personalize that pitch and position what you have to offer as relevant for the proper target, then almost everyone will at least peruse your proposal. The media needs content as much as you need publicity. It's a two-way street, so if you cast your net wide and in a thoughtful fashion, eventually you will offer your content to some editor or producer who needs it at that time as much as you need their attention. Therefore, my objective when creating a publicity campaign is to do everything in my power to create a harmonic convergence, at which point my ideas, intentions, plans, and goals unfold—sometimes by sheer will—and guide me to the right person at the right time. Eventually, one placement leads to another, which triggers another, and things start rolling. Down the line, you'll know that you're doign something right when editors begin e-mailing and calling you, and when television and radio and newspaper folks contact you with so much work that you become stressed! If you actually handle publicity efforts for a living, or are in charge of a publicity department somewhere, then your goal is to create such interest in your product that your phones are ringing off the hook. It's a bit odd, really, because your ultimate goal is to drive yourself crazy, and when you hear the bells and whistles then you know either that you've made it or that you're being driven away in an ambulance.

Don't be intimidated if this seems impossible—transfer any paranoia that you might have into action, and turn any anxiety into excitement. You have the power to fuel this journey, and you must do so in order to reach your goal. Throughout, keep in mind that your work generating publicity is beneficial for everyone involved. Each person needs one another, and everyone gains from the process; it's a win-win-win situation. The person mounting the publicity effort succeeds by securing a booking, the producer or editor receives needed and useful content, and the client gets the publicity attention he or she deserves. In addition, other groups or businesses might also benefit by sheer association. (The theater's production is getting rave reviews, which only helps the restaurant next door, for example.)

I must reiterate that as long as you are professional, and as long as you have content that is truly worthy of your target's time and consideration, you should feel confident that the media needs you as much as you need the media. Otherwise, if your content isn't worthy of dangling in front of others, then leave them alone as you are wasting their time as well as your own.

Keep a piece of paper and a pen with you at all times

To help keep everything involved with your campaign organized, I suggest that you get a journal or notebook that you dedicate to your efforts and in which you keep track of everything in one place. Obviously, you can't bring this journal with you everywhere, but you can keep a pen and paper with you at all times. You never know when a brilliant thought regarding your current publicity effort is going to simply pop into your head, whether it's during your morning walk in the woods with your dog or during your midnight bout with insomnia. Chances are that you will not remember each and every one of these thoughts later, when you are in work mode, so I suggest that you just get in the habit of writing them all down as they occur to you—you could be on the highway, stuck on the subway, or peering into the refrigerator. Jot them all down (or even call your answering machine and record them), and then once a day transcribe any written or recorded thoughts into your master notebook. Not only will this help you stay organized, but it will also allow you to go back and review your thoughts as they

FROM EQUIPMENT TO OFFICE SUPPLIES: WHAT YOU NEED TO ACTUALLY GET STARTED

Fortunately, publicists only need the most basic office tools to be able to research, write, and present themselves and their ideas, in addition to methods of keeping track of notes, information, and media placements. Though they might serve you well if you have them, know that buying all of the latest technological gadgets is not necessary—the biggest tool involved is your mind. Keep the following office equipment in your workspace:

-Answering machine and/or voice mail
-Basic office supplies, from pens to staples
-Calendar with both this year's and next year's dates

-Computer with software programs that at the very least create word-processing documents and simple spreadsheets or databases

-Credit card

-Desk, chair, filing cabinet, and other office furniture

-E-mail account

-Landline phone (a cellular phone is useful, but not absolutely necessary; note that a landline phone is actually necessary to do radio interviews over the phone)

-Notebook or journal

-Postage

-Printer

-Stationery and envelopes for press releases and pitch letter

If you must purchase any of the items mentioned above, be sure to keep all of your receipts for accounting purposes, whether you are submitting them to clients for reimbursement or using them yourself next April for tax deductions

progressively occurred to you—often I find many smaller thoughts seem inconsequential on their own, but trigger ideas later when I see them all together.

Pay attention to what you pay attention to

We are going to take a little test-drive here, so grab your notebook, sit down in front of the television, toss some magazines and newspapers about, and start consuming content. Maybe even grab a watch with a second hand on it so that you can incorporate the concept of time into this self-examination. As you begin to envision how your story needs to be told, and so that you can understand how much content can actually be presented in thirty seconds or one minute, I suggest that you jot down your first impressions in your journal, recording what strikes you.

Start a page listing which media outlets you intrinsically, consciously, and subconsciously allow into your day. Then, think about why. Are they the most popular programs? Is it your choice or your habit, or is it because it's someone else in the house's favorite program? Which programs do you watch? Think about what it is that you read. Which magazines do you subscribe to? Do you have a wide array of publications in your mailbox each month, or none at all? Which radio shows do you listen to? Do you listen to radio only while in the car? How much time do you spend online? What kinds of media do you actually spend money on? In other words: pay attention to what you pay attention to. This will not only help you think as a publicist and sharpen your publicist's instincts, but it will help you understand one key demographic: your own. On another level, while paying attention to what you pay attention to, try to see if you can identify an obviously successful publicity placement. Are efforts made by publicists actually transparent? Look closely at newspaper articles and television and radio news and talk segments, and see if you can distinguish content that a publicist generated. Can you identify information that might very well have been provided by a publicist behind the scenes? Whether you realize it or not, you hear publicity placements every day on the airwaves, and you see the results of publicity campaigns almost every time you turn on the television or pick up a newspaper.

MOST PEOPLE HAVE A PRETTY GOOD UNDERSTANDING OF WHAT ADVERTISING IS, BUT THROUGH THE YEARS, I HAVE FOUND THAT THE WORDS "MARKETING," "PUBLICITY," AND "PROMOTION" ARE CONSTANTLY INTERCHANGED, ONE WORD MISTAKENLY BEING SUBSTITUTED FOR ANOTHER IN CONVERSATIONS. ACTUALLY, THEY ALL HAVE VERY DIFFERENT AND DISTINCT MEANINGS.

Marketing

Think of marketing as the "pie." Publicity, advertising, and promotion are the three pieces of that pie. Whether you want one piece of that pie to be larger than the others, or whether you want three equal-size pieces, there are plenty of ways to slice it.

Publicity

Publicity is free "earned" editorial attention in the form of reviews, or in pieces that mention or feature a product in print, online, or on the air. Publicity is a confluence that usually occurs when a fusion of ideas and instincts are combined with a string of administrative steps in a timely manner. It is not about luck, but I do consider it the riskiest part of the marketing pie, because a lack of control is inherent to the process. The risks are twofold: not only are there no assurances that your desire and effort to generate publicity will actually be achieved, but there are also no assurances that if you actually end up generating publicity, the attention you receive will be favorable.

Sometimes a publicity push is the only piece of a marketing campaign. This is frequently the case when the budget is tight, because publicity can pay huge dividends and can be a really efficient way to allocate marketing dollars. Again, the bottom line regarding publicity is that other than the publicist's time and some of the aforementioned office supplies, essentially there are very little costs involved.

Advertising

Advertising is the creation of a prepared and controlled message that is delivered via purchased page space or airtime. Though advertising is on almost every CEO's wish list, it is "paid media" (rather than "earned media") so it may not be part of every company's budget. On top of that, the costs involved are twofold. First, when the advertisement is conceived, written, and produced, and second when a publication's page space or a television or radio program's airtime or an online banner must be purchased in order to actually place the advertisement in front of the public.

Promotion

Promotion is the creation and distribution of various materials in order to help market a product. The free bookmarks on the checkout desk at your local library, the calendar that your dry cleaner hands out to customers each December, and the navy blue "Springfield Cemetery" sweatshirt that I somehow ended up with at my recent high school reunion's raffle—these are all promotional materials. These create lasting and repeating impressions, but unfortunately they require some cash to create. Such items are not publicity per se, but promotional materials can certainly be, and often are, a great tool to use to generate publicity. They are occasionally even the recipients of publicity themselves.

Thread a stitch of continuity throughout all of the elements of the marketing campaign

When it comes to creating a campaign for your product, remember that publicity is just one piece of the marketing pie. Your effort might be small and personal, and it may be the only piece you have to control, but if advertising and/or promotions are also part of the mix, then make sure you familiarize yourself with the entire marketing campaign. What, if any, advertising copy has already been written for your product? And what promotional materials have already been created on which you can piggyback or in which you can incorporate into your efforts? If such teamwork is part of the blend, then you need to know how the advertising and promotional players are positioning the product and how you can work in tandem with them.

CHAPTER 3 | THINKING OUT OF THE BOX

THROUGHOUT THE COURSE OF MY TWENTY YEARS WORKING AS A PUBLICIST, I HAVE IDENTIFIED AND HONED THE FOLLOWING 7-STEP APPROACH IN ORDER TO COMPREHENSIVELY, SYSTEM-ATICALLY, AND CONFIDENTLY PUBLICIZE JUST ABOUT ANYTHING.

Seven steps to publicize just about anything

STEP 1
START BRAINSTORMING

STEP 2
DISTILL YOUR MESSAGE DOWN TO A CONCENTRATED
REDUCTION

STEP 3
SELECT A SPOKESPERSON

STEP 4
CREATE PRESS MATERIALS

STEP 5
MAP OUT THE STRATEGY

STEP 6
EXECUTE YOUR PLANS

STEP 7
ALLOW YOUR SUCCESS TO PROPEL YOU FORWARD

It certainly can be nerve-wracking and overwhelming when you are beginning to put together a publicity campaign of any sort for the first time, because you don't have the experience to know what to do or when to do it, and so it often feels like you are not doing something that you should be doing, or like you are never doing enough of anything. Instead of taking that approach, I suggest that you use these 7 steps as an overarching guide, and you too will have all of the direction that you will need. Note up front that you will move through some of these steps more quickly than others. I'll now proceed to the fundamentals, breaking down each of the 7 steps into simple and manageable tasks.

STEP 1: Start brainstorming

Conceiving, developing, and implementing a publicity campaign is both a creative process and a business assignment that requires both an artist's vision and a manager's discipline. The fun part of mounting a publicity campaign is immersing yourself in the creative aspects, and to do that, you must free your mind to foster, explore, and indulge its esoteric thoughts, and then, in time, rein it all in so that you can execute the tasks that your unique campaign requires.

Think out of the box

To think out of the box is to allow your imagination to go beyond where your creative thought processes are usually allowed to go. Unless you have some sort of brilliant epiphany regarding your campaign right off the bat, then such an effort will require some time. Brainstorming is tricky, because on the one hand it comes down to instinct, and on the other hand it requires that you tell your mind that it is time to get to work. The bottom line is that it's not going to happen if you don't allow it to and if you don't take the time to do it. This might mean that you need to actually get away from your computer and go for a walk or a swim, or engage in whatever activity it is that enables you to change your pace and your thinking and sweep your mind clean in order to move in a fresh direction. Then, just let it go—start thinking about your campaign, what it needs, what you want from it, how you want to get there, and what you have to work with. Don't limit or edit your thinking.

Am I brainstorming yet?

When you were a child, there were times when your mind was allowed to wander and daydream, but as an adult, the demands of reality often dictate that you move through the day on autopilot. For some, such a scheduled approach to life is simply due to a lack of time, but for others, it is due to fear. Whether because of time constraints or trepidation, we all know people who face life with a rigid, never-deviate-from-the-norm approach, always thinking one particular way, and operating within the confined parameters that they have created and designated for themselves as safe or easy. As a publicist, in contrast, you must work past your fears and begin to think in new ways. To do this, keep a positive attitude and stay upbeat— brainstorming should only be about positive self-talk, and it never includes beating yourself up.

My best brainstorming occurs when I am able to relax long enough for my mind to wander. During these moments, various ideas or solutions to my campaign's challenges come to me. For me, brainstorming has a dream-like quality to it; I enjoy riding its trance-like state, and it reminds me of that delicious morning place between sleep and consciousness, or of childhood days long past when I would stare out the window and imagine all sorts of adventures and entertain all kinds of thoughts. Once, a few years ago, one such brainstorming session produced phantasmagorical results: I conceived the theme for a major event and all its components as I laid on my bed, listening to the rain fall and watching the light shift as water dripped down outside. If I had stifled these thoughts by immediately deciding that it was all too complicated, or too expensive, or too this or too that, the event would never have occurred. So, the bottom line is that you have to allow yourself the time to brainstorm, and you must fuel your imagination and let your mind just think about the task at hand as you begin to explore new thoughts and territory. Just let whatever comes to you come to you, and you can always scale back later if need be. Whatever you do, don't let the cost factors and money issues involved affect your thinking at this stage, as it is not yet time to worry about budget matters—just give yourself permission to let your mind wander and dream, and do so without fear.

Taking it all in

Let's face it, your journey has only just begun, and at this point in the process the end is nowhere in sight! You probably have no idea where to begin, never mind where you are going. So, I suggest that you start thinking about your hooks and angles and options, and looking at the various directions and possibilities that are both obvious and already available to you. All of these options need to be recorded in your notebook, so start a running list. Every product has at least a few publicity angles that can be identified right away, or aspects that might morph into a piece of a campaign or into the entire campaign itself. What are your options if you simply keep your efforts simple and focused? What are the first and most obvious thoughts that pop into your head in terms of publicity? Always begin by exploring your gut instincts, and then try to think those thoughts through, building on them until eventually you begin thinking even bigger and conceiving places you can't even imagine right now.

Letting it sink in

Once you begin brainstorming, you will have some ideas percolating right away. Take a little time to sleep on it and to assess your options, explore the possibilities, and let it all sink in before you begin communicating your thoughts with anyone else involved.

Appeal to the senses

I don't want to suggest that you absolutely must incorporate elements that appeal to and trigger the five senses into your campaign in order for it to be successful, but I do think that as you brainstorm you should at least consider the broad array of sensory possibilities that might exist for you to work with. As publicity efforts rely more and more on technology, it's a great conversation starter for you, and it also offers you a creative way to approach and flesh out the work in front of you. How can the campaign you put together incorporate a way to engage one or all of the senses and bring some texture to the landscape that you create? Think about it: is there a really clever way to incorporate touch, taste, sight, smell, and/or hearing into the publicity process?

Here in Massachusetts, I recently viewed a brief television news segment featuring a museum in Paris mounting an exhibition pairing scents with paintings. I didn't see the exhibit, but it made an impact on me! More than that, though, I imagine that those who actually attended the show now have a subtle sense memory registered in their physical beings that will certainly be remembered for years and that will trigger memories of the museum again in the future, somewhere, sometime. The creator of this exhibit not only provided an unusual sensory experience for those who attended, but also offered a unique opportunity for the museum's publicist.

I recently attended a different art opening, here in the Berkshires in nearby Lenox, and the exhibit included a talented wood-furniture maker whose business card was a thin piece of sanded smoky stained wood the same size as a standard business card. The artist's name and phone number were simply handwritten on it with a thin brush line in black paint. This "out-of-the-box" promotional item delighted me when I found it on the table as a little give-away, so much so that I mentioned it moments later with great enthusiasm when I ran into my septuagenarian neighbor, who also happened to be attending the opening. She bluntly replied, "Calm down, it's a piece of wood with a guy's name on it." So, that said, don't take any of this too seriously, but I recommend that you approach your campaign with sensuality in mind.

Figure out which categories of the media you can target

An important part of the initial brainstorming process—and of the entire publicity process—is to identify which categories of the media your product can dangle a hook to in order to ultimately reach and influence your target audience. Think about sorting through the categories of the media that would consider your product relevant to their world. Begin by matching your product with these various categories until you define which ones are a good fit. Once you have defined your product's target categories, then you will begin to better understand which areas in the media you will be approaching and working with down the road.

The following list offers a sampling of the niche subgroups of the media that exist for you to consider contacting according to how they relate to your product. Certainly, more than one category will be an appropriate match, and a few more may be considered a stretch, but are still worth identifying:

- Advertising
- Antiques
- Architecture
- Art
- Automotive
- Beauty
- Books
- Business
- Design
- Entertainment
- Education
- Environment
- Energy
- Farming
- Fashion
- Film
- Food
- Gardening
- Gift
- Hobbies
- Health and Fitness
- House and Home
- Marketing
- Medical
- Military
- Pets
- Photography
- Real estate
- Religion
- Science
- Sports
- Technology
- Theater
- Toys
- Transportation
- Travel
- Wine and Spirits

There are many other categories, of course, but these are some of the most obvious. Each category is full of magazines, columnists, programs, blogs, and Web sites devoted to that particular topic. Which categories apply to your product? Understanding and identifying such categories allows you to define which magazines are most appropriate to contact, or which editor at a newspaper will most likely be receptive to your pitch. You certainly will not be pitching a sports story to the home editor of your local newspaper; you pitch the sports story to the sports editor. Think about how many of these categories work for you, and then begin to think about categories as they relate to the calendar and your timeline, and so on. The bottom line is that on some level, the categories that your product fits into or relates to, and the nuts and bolts of the content that you have to work with, will very much dictate the direction that your efforts need to take.

After you determine which broad categories are appropriate, search for and begin to consider all of the possible smaller angles contained within those broad groups. Ask yourself what makes your product unique within the context of that category. What are the angles that the category itself dictates that you at least consider? What are the angles that you can consider in order to provide the producers and editors with the seeds of an idea or two? For example, does the cookbook you are publicizing feature a recipe created by a chef at a restaurant in a particular city? If so, point out that fact to the food editor at the newspaper in that market. Some contacts need different pitches than others, so keep in mind that when the time comes, you should offer different hooks to targets in various categories in order to appeal to their unique needs.

Define and explore your target group's demographics
After you have defined what angles you will be touting, start thinking about which segments of the population would most likely be interested in your product, in order to cater your pitch to them. Is it women, or men, or both? Which age group(s)? Is it likely to resonate with single people or married couples? Would your product appeal to a particular religious or ethnic group? You get the idea—do your research and begin to define the demographics. It's your due diligence.

Once you have done your homework, it can only help the cause to dig a little deeper. For example, if you decide that demographics dictate that your target group is retired people, then look into how many retired people there are in the relevant geographic areas. Try to determine if answers to the following types of questions will help your publicity efforts:

-Where do the most retired people reside?

-What is the best way to reach them?

-What do they read? What do they watch on television?

-How many women are retired and alive and well versus men?

The bottom line is that part of the gig requires that you ask some questions and immerse yourself in the answers.

Follow your instincts

Listen carefully to what your gut is telling you. Whenever I complete a campaign, I take a moment to go through that campaign's notebook to make sure that there are no loose ends that I forgot about along the way. This inevitably takes me down memory lane, but for the first time, I know how the journey ended. The impression I most often take away from this exercise is how accurate my gut instincts were to start with, in addition to throughout the process.

When I worked at Chronicle Books in San Francisco, I once publicized a book of poetry written to help individuals deal with the process of grieving. Written by Hugh Shurley, *The Ribbon* is an unusually designed title that is almost as much a decoration as it is a book. It uses a kite being swept away by the wind as a metaphor for the struggles of letting a loved one go to AIDS. Until that point in my career, I had never worked with poetry as a genre, so that made the project a little intimidating for me, and the sensitivity the topic required made me a little self-conscious as well. The fact that folks don't often flock to the poetry aisle didn't make things any easier, so I knew in my gut that I had to brainstorm and find a way for this special project to shine. My instincts told me to approach the management of the San Francisco AIDS Foundation to suggest that they consider using the book and its kite image as the theme for an event, just when they happened to be looking for a theme for that year's San Francisco AIDS Foundation Leadership Recognition Dinner. When they accepted, I decided then and there that listening to one's inner voice is a crucial and a powerful tool.

Together, the foundation and I brainstormed and orchestrated an event that occurred just prior to the annual dinner. We enlisted fifty or sixty volunteers to fly white kites aloft in the sky above the event's entrance, highlighted by the nearby San Francisco Bay's majestic blue waters in the background, just as hundreds of the nonprofit's loyal donors and luminaries entered into the warehouse on the marina that was hosting the function. Inside, the kite metaphor was used everywhere, from projected images on the stage and centerpieces on the dining tables to the advertisements in promotional booklets produced for people to take home with them. Fortunately for all involved, not only did the promotional and advertising departments piggyback on the theme, but various members of the press took notice, from newspaper photographers to television stations, and they all came to the event and captured its soaring images on film. Due to the incredible efforts of the foundation, as well as the spirit of my colleagues at the publishing house, the evening's event went on to raise more than one million dollars, and hopefully the publicity also helped everyone involved. Listening to my instincts gave me one of the most gratifying work experiences that I have been involved with to date, and, more importantly, it offered the ideas and angles that I needed in order to successfully accomplish my job as the book's publicist.

National versus local media outlets

In the past, media placements were pretty much considered either national or regional bookings, and that is essentially still the case today. At the same time, the line between the two is blurring, as technology makes local news available globally at the push of a button. An author I recently worked with conducted a phone interview with a Great Barrington, Massachusetts, radio program from her apartment in New York and then hopped on an airplane for Dubai. Only after she arrived at her hotel on the other side of the world was she able to finally listen to her interview online.

Consider and weigh the various national versus regional hooks that you have before you, and make sure you are rolling forward and considering targets on both fronts. Eventually, you will need to distinguish how many national contacts you are approaching from how many regional pitches. National news reaches every region of the country, and therefore has the potential to connect with a huge segment of the nation's population. Free network television programs such as the top-rated morning programs are good examples of a national publicity placement opportunity that has the potential to reach a huge portion of the population all at once. Of course, the competition for these programs' producers' attention is fierce, because every other publicist in the country is also contacting them.

A customized local angle for a regional pitch often requires a more personalized hook than a pitch to a national target, which is meant to appeal to the masses. You might consider approaching an editor at a major magazine or a producer at a national news program with a "what-everyone-needs-to-know" angle, whereas you might consider pitching your own local newspaper with a "hometown boy/girl does good" local angle. When I worked with Los Angeles–based fitness and nutrition expert Robert Reames a few years ago to publicize his book, *Make Over Your Metabolism*, I booked him for a segment on CBS's *Early Show* after pitching his wise and healthy advice that is certainly useful to one and all, but I sent a much more personalized local pitch to his hometown television targets in Indiana.

Cable and satellite television are also powerful venues, though of course they only reach households that pay for such services. They offer a myriad of choices, many created to entertain the masses, while other programming is created to delight very targeted niche audiences—essentially, there is programming that needs content in every category listed on page 33. Regional media can be considered more accessible than national media, though, because it's local and because it's there in part to give a voice to the community and its interests in one particular urban, suburban, or rural area.

Market research

There are corporations, politicians, and all kinds of people who hire market-research firms and/or create focus groups when developing or launching a product. Such efforts usually entail assembling a table full of individuals in target demographics, and the company in question acquires the opinions and tastes of those in attendance. I realize that you are probably not about to retain an agency to orchestrate such an event for your product, but I do suggest that you borrow the basic concept that focus groups employ by seeking out the opinions that you can find, one by one, and learning from the market-research results that grassroots conversations offer. I'm talking about generating informal and unscientific discussions around your own kitchen table or with a stranger on the bus. Search for and gather the opinions of those you trust and those around you. Whether you are asking local sales people direct questions about how this or that product is selling or about what their opinions are concerning certain trends in business, or whether you are asking the local taxi driver a few questions on the way to the airport, gathering such input can be very helpful and very informative.

Never assume anything

Never assume that the product that you are publicizing will definitely get the attention you are seeking from any source just because you or one of your colleagues have deemed the placement a "natural." The mathematics involved will almost always offer a range of possible outcomes, and both sides of the success spectrum are sure to be experienced. This is one reason that a publicist should never take anything for granted when attempting to generate publicity. Sometimes stuff just doesn't happen on your schedule. Always be hopeful and optimistic about the possibilities, but at the same time you must reel in your team's expectations from the start; don't allow them to be arrogant or naïve by assuming the publicity placement will be made. The fact that the product seems like a perfect fit does not automatically translate into ink or airtime.

There are times, due to a whole host of likely and unlikely reasons, that more will be involved behind the scenes than you can possibly be aware of. You might be denied media attention for a good reason. For example, the most likely magazine target you can think of may have just completed a story similar to the one you are pitching. Or something completely unpredictable might prevent your placement, as when an art director nixes your product's inclusion in a magazine because your product's packaging doesn't work well with the color scheme that the art department is trying to weave throughout the issue. Whatever the case may be, there could be any number of reasons unbeknownst to you that the most perfect media outlet informs you that they are "passing." Actually, more often than not, they never tell you anything at all, so be cognizant and appreciative of any communication whatsoever from editors and producers. Your pitch may certainly be worth the attention of a magazine editor, but that doesn't mean you will get ink, and if you are getting ink, that doesn't necessarily mean that anyone will even tell you! (Hence, the importance of following up, which I will discuss in Chapter 8.)

Dedicate a calendar to the cause

In my opinion, it is best to orchestrate a publicity campaign in layers, methodically and step by step. Work performed today hopefully leads to one layer of attention in the future, and next week's effort leads to an additional layer, with wave upon wave of publicity attention rolling in. To do this you not only need a journal, but you need to create a master calendar.

Create a timeline

With your calendar in hand, you can begin to create your campaign's timeline as well as a schedule for yourself that maps out not only what your plans are and the dates of specific events, but also deadlines for when you must get everything done. Publicity is complicated in the sense that you must always be busy and deal with today's to-do list and office demands, but at the same time you must constantly think ahead about what is coming down the road and perform the tasks now that are relevant to those future endeavors. You have to think about the press release that needs to go out this afternoon, in addition to devoting some attention to the party planned for next month.

Get key *personal* dates on the calendar

First things first: If your publicity efforts are going to be long-term, then I suggest that the very first dates you enter on the calendar be your personal dates. Events that punctuate your life—your long-planned trip to Paris next May, your child's birthday, or other important celebrations—should be blocked off from the get-go.

Get key *work* dates on the calendar

Take a step back and look at the obvious dates involved in your endeavor. Record all the information you already have, such as relevant deadlines and other calendar entries. Then, look at the agenda again with your publicist hat on, and for publicity purposes work backward on the calendar. In order to ensure goals are achieved in the campaign, you have to look at the schedule and decide what gets done and when. From the date at which you want to begin contacting the press (often up to six months in advance for the longest-lead magazines), to the amount of time you will need in order to create press materials, to how much time it will take to build a Web site, you must begin carefully and thoughtfully mapping it all out with a calendar in hand. It is imperative to work as far in advance as possible because, as I often say, "next year is like tomorrow," in terms of working with magazines and television programs with long lead times (I will explore lead times more in Chapter 7). Prior to contacting them, you should build time into the schedule to brainstorm, create databases and press materials, and get physically organized and mentally prepared to push forward.

Now that the obvious dates are recorded, start identifying the dates you must designate for your campaign to use to generate publicity. Are you an upstart about to open your doors for the first time? Is your existing business about to celebrate an anniversary? Are you going to stage a special event? Brainstorm and figure out when your product will be available, what you have to celebrate, and what role history has to play. Once you determine your options, then decide what the best plan is for your campaign, and work toward using the dates consistent with that plan and with the work that must be done in advance. Place these dates on the calendar as the major temporal cornerstones of your publicity campaign.

Conventions

Consider adding your industry's annual convention to your yearly calendar. If your publicity effort is for a local shoe store, then you should attend the annual shoe show; if you are representing an author, go to the publishing industry's annual convention. Attend the events with a publicist's perspective. Build into the calendar the work you need to do in advance, such as researching events at the convention, signing up for seminars that you would like to attend, booking appointments with others in attendance, etc. Work the floor to do a little market research of your own, and observe how your colleagues are handling their own publicity efforts.

Keep an eye on the long haul

Take a look at your campaign with a long-term view in mind. What might be happening next year or the year after in your industry or on the world stage that might be relevant? If you are the publicist for a sporting goods company, then maybe you should consider looking at the company's publicity campaign with respect to the next few Olympic Games on the calendar. Any date around which you can revolve a campaign's theme, or which you can piggyback on in some way, should be on your calendar.

In addition, you should ask yourself which seasons of the year offer hooks that might work for you. Aside from your initial launch, look to the calendar to see if you can create future waves of attention, allowing you to reach out to writers seeking content for stories with calendar themes. Experts and content are needed for all types of yearly dates and occasions, from January's New Year's resolutions ("It's the First Day of the Rest of Your Life" stories) to December's holiday gift-giving wrap-up articles.

Know that there are a number of functions you can schedule and special events that you can create for publicity purposes. Some may work for your needs and efforts, and some may not, but it's good to be aware of the possibilities. Whichever event you decide to create or partake in, remember to record the date in your calendar, and then work backward. There will be a hundred and one things to attend to, including locations, sound systems, invitations, and/or goody-filled gift bags for distribution. Each component of the publicity-generating event creates not only work, but bills as well—but when it's right, it's right.

Here are some examples of potential events/occasions you could organize:

Opening day
When you want to draw a line in the sand, consider scheduling an "opening day" as the official start date for the product you are publicizing. Whether it's for a theater production's three-week engagement, a new restaurant with long-term potential, a retail shop taking over a store front in a strip mall, or an amusement park's annual kickoff, opening day is an obvious angle to consider employing for publicity purposes.

Release date

Many products, from books to gadgets, schedule distribution very carefully, and that process offers a very specific "release date" to work with: the day that the product is actually available to be released to the public. When relevant, this is the perfect opportunity and very much a classic scenario when it comes to producing publicity.

Happy anniversary

This may at times be a challenge as far as publicity goes, but adding a little ritual to the mix never hurt anyone. Whether you are publicizing a restaurant celebrating thirty years in business, or an actor celebrating his or her third anniversary on a successful situation comedy, I urge you to consider giving a nod to the past as you move toward the future. You might recall how much press attention the garment industry recently received as they celebrated the one hundredth anniversary of the bra. Let's face it—some publicist somewhere did some serious brainstorming to come up with that!

Launch parties

Planning launch parties to celebrate new products or new releases can take months of preparation, so it is best to start planning them as early as possible, and to get the date on your (and everyone else's) calendar as soon as you can. Even if you have never been in charge of such a special event before, you can organize a great launch event if you handle things step by step. First and foremost, secure the perfect space as far in advance as possible. Once the space is booked, you can add on all of the other layers according to what that space can accommodate.

In addition to goodwill, word-of-mouth benefits, and the networking opportunities that such events generate, launch parties offer the publicist another opportunity to reach out to the press and extend an invitation. Frankly, you can host a launch event just about anywhere and with just about any budget. I have put together large-scale events with essentially no budget, and, on the other hand, I once hosted a launch event in Manhattan for a book and had a $100,000 budget just for the party. Launch parties can take many forms: You can toss a regular, good-old party with a bar and hors d'oeuvres; you can dream up some type of unusual "happening" or special event; or you can put together a simple wine-and-cheese table and a bouquet of flowers just about anywhere. Parties can be held in large halls, private homes, or at venues such as local galleries or restaurants. Continue thinking out of the box.

Upscale retail environments can often be persuaded to donate their spaces for no fee, because events deliver potential new customers to their door, as well as offer the vendors the possibility of being included in the publicity that you generate. If you do host a party in a retail store, let me suggest that you serve only white wine, as you know that otherwise some sloppy guest will spill red wine on a wall or a rack of clothes.

That said, if you serve alcohol, you should be very prudent regarding its distribution and how much your bartender is allowed to serve your guests. Always have plenty of nonalcoholic beverages available and at least one snack in case people need a little something to nibble on.

A "National Media Day"

If you expect that your product has the potential to make a splash on the national scene, you may want to consider designating a particular kickoff date and declaring it as "National Media Day," as you line up a string of interviews, events, and appearances in a block of time on that day. The date might be very obvious because it's the first date your product is available or the first day your new establishment is open, but if not, you might consider tying it in to an anniversary or another sentimental date on the calendar. The bottom line is to pick a date (after seeking input from everyone involved on your team) and to declare that one day to be your National Media Day.

A press conference

Press conferences are only appropriate when you have a major announcement or a big, important message that is best delivered in a timely and controlled manner. Ideally, press conferences distribute information in a very fair and balanced way, as everyone gets to hear the announcement at the same time. They might at first seem overwhelming to orchestrate, but they really are pretty simple to conduct. Someone makes an introduction, someone makes an announcement worthy of the press's attention, and then a period of time is designated

Press conference checklist:

-Box of facial tissues on stage

-Lighting (if necessary)-

-Member of your team
positioned at the entrance
with a guest list

-Microphone and sound
equipment

-Pen and pad on podium

-Photographer (and possibly
videographer)

-Podium or table and chairs

-Security (if necessary)

-Water

for questions and answers. It's not the event itself that's the challenge; in my opinion, the real challenge is getting the press to confirm that they will attend prior to the event. On the one hand, you do not want to hold a press conference unless you have substantial information to deliver, and on the other hand, there is no use holding a press conference if you can't get any press to show up, so don't let your ego or a controlling colleague persuade you to hold a press conference if the news you have to announce does not warrant one.

I recently received an e-mail from an author's assistant seeking some advice regarding how to hold a press conference, and she wondered how far in advance she should send the media an advisory regarding the upcoming event, and what she should have at the press conference for handouts. She wrote me the e-mail on the tenth of the month, and the press conference was scheduled for just over two weeks later, on the twenty-sixth. I replied, "Focus on the media alert first, as well as the invite list, and start getting those out immediately. Then, begin following up with everyone you target to make sure the advisory landed on their radar screens, and keep track of who you talked to and who confirmed that they would attend. In the meantime, compile enough of your own press kits and contact the publisher to get copies of the book to give out to all in attendance."

If a press conference is part of your plans, then you should hire a photographer to document the event itself. Request that the photographer shoot both black-and-white and color images, so that you have photography that meets the varying needs of different outlets. By doing this, you use the conference itself not only to announce your message, but also to publicize it. Hiring a photographer will also help you sleep better the night before, as you can rest assured that at least one person in the room will be devoted to capturing images of the event while it is happening. That way, if someone requests an image a week later, you can respond to the request immediately because you control the rights to share the photography. In addition, consider shooting the event on video, if that is within your means, so that you will also have footage to distribute.

Tie in to what the calendar itself offers

The calendar on page 51 lists many of the dates and cyclical themes that might offer appropriate hooks for your publicity efforts. Many businesses take advantage of these merchandising themes annually, and you should at least consider how the calendar's offerings might inherently work for your publicity campaign.

There are many other dates and themes that you can take advantage of; this illustration could go on forever. My suggestion is to let the calendar give you some ideas, if not some answers, regarding ways to proceed.

A friend of mine owns a bed-and-breakfast, and she mentioned recently that her business booms in the summer and in the fall but slows down in the winter and spring. I suggested that she take a look at the calendar to see if it offered any ideas for generating publicity about her inn in the off-season. I also recommended that she consider how she might use the calendar not only to generate ink at that time, but also as a tool to examine how she can piggyback with things going on in the area in the off-season and align herself with the needs of local businesses and nonprofits. For example, there are two small ski resorts within ten minutes of the inn that she could connect with to create a ski-and-lodging package deal to help draw guests in the winter. She could then publicize that effort. In addition, the Berkshire International Film Festival is staged in the region each spring, and that event might offer a marketing opportunity when the snow begins to melt. The point is to give the calendar some focus and to ask yourself what it tells you.

Other publicity opportunities might be as simple as plugging into the days of the week. For example, Tuesday is considered the quietest day to shop at a grocery store, Wednesdays are the day of the week that newspapers designate for weekly food sections in most markets across the country, and Fridays boast the weekend event calendars in local newspapers. Consider how using a particular day of the week for your calendared event might be advantageous.

JANUARY

- New Year's resolutions
- Winter (nesting, hearth, and home)
- Post-holiday bills (post-holiday blues)
- Martin Luther King, Jr.'s birthday
- National Mentoring Month

FEBRUARY

- Valentine's Day
- Presidents' Day
- Black History Month

MARCH

- St. Patrick's Day
- Spring (gardening and preparing for the season)
- National Women's History Month

APRIL

- April Fools' Day
- Earth Day
- Passover
- Easter
- Arbor Day
- Baseball

MAY

- May Day
- Cinco de Mayo
- Mother's Day
- Nurse's Day
- National Teachers Day
- National Poetry Month
- Graduation
- Memorial Day

JUNE

- Father's Day
- World Refugee Day
- Summer Solstice
- Summer travel/beach reading
- World Environment Day
- Gay & Lesbian Pride Day

JULY

- Independence Day
- Summer sidewalk sales

AUGUST

- Back to school
- National Aviation Day
- Tag sales

SEPTEMBER

- Labor Day
- Grandparents Day
- Native American Day
- Prostate Cancer Awareness Month

OCTOBER

- Fall foliage
- Halloween
- World Series
- National Breast Cancer Awareness Month

NOVEMBER

- Elections
- Veterans Day
- Thanksgiving

DECEMBER

- Human Rights Day
- Christmas
- Hanukkah
- Kwanzaa

STEP 2: Distill your message down to a concentrated reduction

WHEN YOU BEGIN TO INTERACT WITH THE PRESS, THERE WILL BE TIMES WHEN YOU HAVE ALL THE TIME IN THE WORLD TO DELIVER YOUR PITCH, AND THERE WILL BE TIMES WHEN YOU HAVE AN EDITOR'S EAR OR A PRODUCER'S ATTENTION FOR LITERALLY ONLY A MATTER OF SECONDS. Whatever the case, you need to be able to sum it all up quickly and hit the nail on the head for however long you hold their interest. In order to effectively communicate your message during the pitch, it is crucial that you craft, in advance, one powerful sentence that sums everything up regarding your product. This is what I like to call "distilling your message down to a concentrated reduction." Not only is this concentrated reduction useful to you as you pitch the product, but it will also be a handy sound bite for the spokesperson during interviews and conversations later on.

When attempting to find the words to sum up your product in one sentence and distill your handle(s) down to the bare bones, consider all of the reasons this product is relevant to the member of the press you will approach. This task is often easier said than done, and many of you will find this step harder than you expected from reading this short chapter!

Often, a product represents so much more than can possibly be described in one sentence. That is, until you focus and get down to business. Button up your pitch now so that others can do so as well throughout the campaign. How can you expect your product to be touted or pitched efficiently by others if you can't spit it out yourself? Individuals, from salespeople to newspaper editors to talk show producers all need a quick, intelligent, and concentrated reduction when being pitched, and then again when they, in turn, deliver your message. Make it as easy as possible for them, at the same time giving yourself maximum control over the message.

To accomplish this task, you again might have to take a step back in order to access the whole of your campaign, and only then will you be able to wrap it all up in a succinct little package. Hone down and focus on the key angles and selling points that exist, and then prioritize them. Trust your instincts, allow yourself to proceed, and think about the small stuff and the big stuff. Meld them all together to make one statement. An easy-to-understand distillation is most often prudent, and that takes editing, and more editing, which takes time.

The very first campaign I put together on my own was for a photography book by Georg Gerster entitled *Amber Waves of Grain*. Looking back, I would say that the book's concentrated reduction might have been something like, "*Amber Waves of Grain* is a photography book featuring America's farmlands from above as seen by one of the world's leading aerial photographers." Strip everything down to the bare bones and come up with a simple, easy, inclusive, and to-the-point sentence.

The concentrated reduction for this book, the one you are currently reading, is basically built into the title and subtitle. When the time comes to talk about it, I anticipate that I will say something like, "*Publicity* offers anyone anywhere an organized approach to publicize just about anything . . ." Of course, this is what comes to me today as I write this, but believe me, I am not married to these words, and nor should you be to your words while your campaign is in its developing stages. I always want to keep things fresh, and maybe in a year I will be saying something completely different. Stay open, because it makes the process fluid.

From this point forward, your concentrated reduction will be a key piece of ammunition and an empowering marketing and sales tool for everyone involved in the publicity process. Such a simple approach to the big story pays off, because as you distill your message down to the basics, and as you discover and prioritize a variety of useful angles, points, and anecdotes, you will determine which ones are crucial to convey and which are not. Such a sound bite will come in handy and serve you well during a pitch or an interview. You will have the confidence of knowing your miniscript is on the tip of your tongue, waiting to be uttered at the perfect opportunity.

STEP 3: Select the spokesperson

EVERY PRODUCT POSITIONED FOR PUBLICITY PURPOSES SHOULD HAVE A DESIGNATED SPOKESPERSON ATTACHED TO IT TO SERVE AS THE CAMPAIGN'S VOICE. WITHOUT A SPOKESPERSON, THE PRODUCT ITSELF MIGHT VERY WELL RECEIVE SOME COVERAGE AND BE SHOWCASED IN THE PRESS, BUT CHANCES ARE, IF YOU HAVE A TALKING HEAD ATTACHED TO YOUR PRODUCT, YOU WILL END UP WITH MORE PUBLICITY. This is because that person literally and physically becomes a tool for you to work with, giving you another hook to dangle in front of the press in order to entice them to cover your product. Then, when you actually secure the article or interview for your product, the story will get longer coverage and convey more key points because the spokesperson made a human connection and was able to flesh things out.

More often than not, I pitch the media a product with only one on-air spokesperson attached. For many reasons, including organizational, budgetary, and branding purposes, I suggest that you keep it simple and streamlined by designating one person as the official spokesperson for any given campaign.

The publicist thus offers the media one qualified voice, available to represent the product. In addition, the media often prefers being pitched just one person. I remember working on a book a few years ago that involved two male authors. When I booked a segment on a radio show and offered the producer both men for the program, I was asked to select one or the other, because the station's policy was to avoid booking two guests on the same show as part of the same segment, for fear that their listeners would not know which guest was talking.

If you are publicizing a novel that an author spent years writing, then the choice of the spokesperson to publicize the book is obvious: the author him or herself. But it isn't always that easy. Often, a number of people are behind a product or artistic endeavor. Whoever is top dog must either be the spokesperson (the one to deliver the streamlined messages) or decide who will be designated as such. Egos might get involved, and if they do, the process is a bit like politics: that which is best for the majority takes precedence over that which is best for the individual. The secondary player should step aside, and in turn the designated spokesperson should be generous and give credit where credit is due, acknowledging the efforts of all involved.

However, large-scale efforts with various marketing strategies, geographics, and/or logistics may require a few different individuals as spokespeople, like Mr. Apple in Manhattan or Ms. Orange in Los Angeles, for example. Though it's more work for you, you can designate one person as spokesperson in each separate market, and then select a voice to handle the nationals. In addition, there are times when it is necessary and appropriate for different individuals to fan out and cover different regions. But when you are just getting the ball rolling, you will have the most control if you keep things focused and work with only one spokesperson.

Personality is really important

Your product or its main theme can be backed by years of study, research, writing, funding, development, dreams, and imagination, but when it comes time for the spokesperson to look into the camera lens, all of that research and hard work can in one moment become secondary to the spokesperson's personality, or lack thereof. The spokesperson must possess the confidence to harness the creative forces at work, and the social skills required to be an intelligent and spontaneous conversationalist on command, while at the same time listening and coming across as an authority. He or she should never attempt to be a caricature of an expectation. One doesn't have to be beautiful to be a spokesperson, nor does one have to look like an academic, but one does have to be oneself, and sincere and comfortable in one's own skin.

THE WORD DU JOUR

Back in the '90s, when I wrote the first draft of this book, it seemed to me that the word du jour in the corporate world was "synergy," as currencies, industries, and companies the globe over were working together and merging. Now, ten years later, the hot word I keep hearing over and over is "platform." Just the other day, my publisher asked me to describe my platform for this book. Whether you are an individual or a corporation, building a platform and working across platforms is now a necessity in business.

My publisher asked about my platform because she needs to inform the sales force of whatever built-in audience I bring along as potential customers. To have a platform, an author doesn't have to be as celebrated as J. K. Rowling, with a loyal following and fans lined up around the block the moment an embargo is lifted and the book is released. Rather, having a platform simply implies that the individual has some vehicle in place to help him or her get the word out about their product. Whether the product is a book written by a syndicated columnist who also has a blog; or a new granola line created by a celebrated pastry chef with a very successful bakery, Web site, extensive mailing list, and loyal following; or a primer on publicity written by a man with a very large Irish family—it has a platform to stand on. Begin examining, defining, and enhancing the components of your platform, whatever it might be.

Know your competition

Once the spokesperson is designated, both you and that individual must begin to get to know the competition because the spokesperson must always work to elevate your product above the rest of the pack. Who else, or what else, exists out there in the marketplace, competing with you for the same page space and airtime? It might make you nervous to even think about, or even crazy and more aggressive when you suddenly notice your competitors and something they are doing well. If you are a publicist at a publishing house, look at the editor's notes about the competition and research other books that might compete with the new book you are touting. If you are a caterer with a new business, survey the phone book and the Internet for information regarding the other businesses in town. The bottom line is you must get real about the competition.

Once you have a list of competitors, start looking at how (or if) they market and publicize themselves. What is their look? What is the hook, if any, that they are using to market their product? Do they publicize, advertise, or utilize promotional materials? Now consider how you might be able to differentiate your product from the competition and set it apart from the others. Keep in mind that the elements you are seeking to emphasize to make your product distinctive can be found anywhere, from price points to package design to publicity execution. Is your pitch positioning your product as the experienced, long-time leader, or as the new hot thing? Often the most compelling angle is the simplest—for example, the unique human story behind the scenes.

When it comes to actually having to generate publicity, the factors that you can never control are 1) the quantity of the existing competition and 2) when your competitors will raise their ugly heads. They exist everywhere, not just in your field and the categories of media you are targeting; there is a huge amount of competition out there in general, and there is only so much sexy media within which to publicize it. Also, the landscape continually changes and evolves. For example, there are fewer and fewer book review sections in major metropolitan newspapers, and thus more competition for the page space they offer. And there are only so many segments that the *Today Show*'s producers can create in a year. Everyone everywhere is playing the same big game, vying for the same space on the published page and the same minute on the airwaves. So, take the time to understand the competition and take even greater care determining what sets your product apart.

Keep your eyes on the headlines

The publicist and the spokesperson should always keep current and read various daily newspapers, peruse Web sites and blogs, and watch the news every day, keeping their eyes and ears open to what's going on in the world. Always seek new hooks, news angles, and bits of conversation that will make your pitch and your product as current and as relevant as possible. Keeping up with the national and international news gives the publicist target ideas as well. You might very well be surprised by how often the news triggers an idea, or offers information that will in some way support your efforts. What is happening in the world that relates to your product, mission, and goals? If worse comes to worst, keeping up with the news will not help your specific work, but will help you in general, as it is part of your job to keep your finger on the media pulse and to be an informed publicist with the confidence and fodder to talk to anyone.

Media training

Media training offers a spokesperson the opportunity to think about key points and messages that must be driven home in the course of an interview. The exercise offers the tools to equip the spokesperson to do just that with anecdotes, eye contact, and confidence. In the '90s, when I worked as a publicist at Chronicle Books in San Francisco, I was booked to be a guest on Joan Rivers's national television shopping/talk show to promote a series of books written by a number of different people. These authors were subcontracted by a book packager, and unfortunately when the booking occurred there wasn't one designated spokesperson in place, so off to the airport I went.

Before the day of the interview arrived, I was quite confident that doing the television program would be a breeze, because since college I have worked a little bit in New York and Hollywood on both sides of the camera. But I have to tell you, I was very intimidated from the minute I arrived at the television studio in Manhattan. Standing backstage with knees shaking, I realized that I was about to go on the air with an American comic icon, and not only did I feel humorless, but I suddenly completely lost my confidence as well as my concentration— my memory seemed to disappear. I can remember standing all alone backstage in the wings of the set just before I was introduced, wondering why was I putting myself under so much pressure. In acting, dialogue is scripted, and you get to rehearse. However, talk shows are not usually scripted, so guests have no idea what is going to be discussed next. As I stood there and pondered the possibilities, I began to panic and became certain that Ms. Rivers was going to ask me questions for which I had no answers.

Once my talk-show interview began, I was so nervous that I froze and found it hard to engage in conversation. I basically let my host take over, and I just kept saying the words, "Indeed, Joan," over and over again! I simply tanked; I honestly think I said, "Indeed, Joan," about fifteen times in a quick three- or four-minute segment. Ultimately, I failed because I had never appeared live on a national television talk show before, and I had no media training whatsoever. If I had a little more experience or if I had done even a little homework before I hopped on the plane, I would have had a better idea of how to control myself before, during, and after the interview. I would have had the concentration to engage with my host during the interview and to inject message-driven dialogue regarding my product throughout the segment.

So, an inexperienced spokesperson shouldn't be insulted if

someone on the team suggests that he or she receive some media training, as that need is certainly nothing to be embarrassed about. Believe me, it's more embarrassing not to have media training than it is to have media training. Media training provides the spokesperson with the tools and the mentality needed to succeed in front of the camera or microphone with confidence, and to interact with the print and broadcast media with flair.

During the course of a media training session, a spokesperson rehearses various interview scenarios to acquire and practice the techniques necessary to succeed. Once you have a little media training under your belt, you will have a new understanding of how to listen as well as of how the give-and-take aspect of an interview works. This will allow you to begin to explore various approaches to different aspects of the interview process. You will learn to understand both the big picture and various nuances, and you will become skilled in plugging what you need to plug while deflecting what you don't want to talk about. In addition, you will be trained to look at things from the interviewer's perspective in order to predict questions. Ultimately, the individual with media training under his or her belt will soon possess more confidence and become a better interviewee.

Because of the costs involved, most spokespeople who could use a little media training will not have the luxury of working with a professional media training coach, but there are activities that you can do on your own to practice and help you prepare. One benefit of media training is that it allows the trainee the opportunity to observe him or herself on camera and to discover what he or she does well, as well as to reveal his or her assets and idiosyncrasies. While working with a media coach for an intense block of time, you should expect to spend time practicing mock interviews in front of a camera or microphone in a safe environment. You will work to develop and shape content and to deliver that content thoughtfully, and you will practice breathing, timing, and eye contact. Even the most experienced performers get nervous when the camera is rolling and have butterflies before, during, and sometimes even after an appearance, so don't be surprised if you and the spokesperson do, too. A little confidence boosting can only help.

If attending media training is just not in the cards, then I suggest that you or your spokesperson always make sure to listen carefully to an interviewer's questions, stay in the moment, and go with the flow to allow the spontaneity involved to unfold. Fewer surprises will occur if you practice mock interviews with your spokesperson in front of a video camera, computer, or with a tape recorder. Write some obvious questions in your journal, and record your spokesperson answering them, playing back the interview when finished to see or hear how well they responded. Does the spokesperson talk too much about details that are not key components of your message and concentrated reduction? Did he or she talk enough? Did he or she get in a plug for your product? Can that plug be enhanced or better crafted? Was the spokesperson able to get in more than one plug?

Finally, I suggest that you or your spokesperson get physical. Start by standing in front of the mirror and exercising your facial muscles by stretching your face this way and that way. Start in the center with the nose and contort the facial features up, down, left, and right. Then, try relaxing your face, followed by stretching and loosening up your shoulders, back, and entire body. Always perform these exercises before an appearance, so that you or your spokesperson are as relaxed and confident as can be. Additionally, simple vocal exercises will help loosen up a nervous voice before interviews.

STEP 4: Create press materials

AS I HAVE SAID BEFORE, THE PRESS IS IN THE CONTENT-DELIVERY BUSINESS, AND UNTIL RECENTLY THE ONE MANDATORY DOCUMENT IN ANY STANDARD PUBLICITY CAMPAIGN WAS THE PRESS RELEASE (SOMETIMES CALLED A NEWS RELEASE). The press release, your essential stand-alone master document, is used to alert the press that you are seeking coverage. Whether sent by mail, messenger, fax, or e-mail, the press release positions the news and information that you have to share with reporters, editors, and producers in a ready-to-print (in a publication) or ready-to-read (on the air) format. You can also provide the press with a bio or materials, such as facts and figures or questions and answers, all as part of a press kit. However, all documents other than the press release are optional.

Press release

A friend of mine, a freelance artist and fashion designer, recently stated that she wanted to get some publicity to help her acquire some more work. I piped in immediately and offered to help her write a press release to achieve her goal.

I was surprised when she looked at me, utterly perplexed, and exclaimed, "Why on earth would I need a press release to get publicity?" The answer to that question is that a press release, along with a cover letter (and possibly a sample product, if there is one) has always been the most basic tool you have to work with to get publicity, no matter what is being publicized. I believe my friend was so puzzled when I mentioned that I would help her write a press release because she was under the assumption that such documents were only distributed when a person or company had breaking news to share, but in essence, the press release does just that. It "releases" your news to the press, whatever your news may be.

How to begin writing a press release

The idea of writing a press release is always much more frightening to me than the actual task itself. Frankly, I feel most vulnerable when I learn that I have to write a press release for some big-shot author's book, and before I send it out to even one reporter, my final draft must pass by the author for his or her approval. The fact is, whether you like it or not, you have to write press materials to get publicity for your product, and it's important that you do it well. Following is how I begin the process of writing the press release for anything or anyone I am publicizing.

First, I create a master document for the release on my computer and begin brainstorming, referring to my journal. I quickly write down all of my thoughts about the product in a loose stream-of-consciousness form, one thought after the other, jotting down everything that comes to mind that I feel

I might want to get across in the release. I am at this point not concerned about my writing style or sentence structure; I am simply focused on getting all of the relevant thoughts out of my head and onto the page. Then, I refer to any existing materials that might have been provided to me by colleagues involved in the project. These may include menus, a book jacket's flap copy, or preexisting product descriptions. I add all of the pertinent details and information to my document. Then I refer to the product itself, choosing a couple of key aspects—my favorite excerpt from a book, my favorite recipe from a restaurant, or any other special nugget of content. I hunt and gather appropriate content until I have enough thoughts on the page to give some shape to the tone of the document.

In time, my job becomes editing more than writing, as I arrange and craft my content. I try to start off with an engaging first sentence—a hook—and then attempt to arch the who, what, when, where, and why facts into a compelling sequence of events. Every aspect of this sequence should contain information that is credible and sincere. Write the page, then edit the page, and then rewrite the page over and over, continuing to do so until you have crafted and edited the document that you desire. Your press release should contain three fundamental paragraphs at the very least: a beginning, a middle, and an end. The following must also appear in your release:

-Your contact information (contact name, phone, and e-mail address)
-Headline
-Opening paragraph

-Main paragraph

-Closing paragraph

-Bio (If not a separate document after the release, then include a few sentences)

-Specifications (In publishing, this includes information about the book: how many pages, paperback or hardcover, etc. If you are touting another business, this is where you might want to list the address, phone, fax, Web site, etc.)

Ultimately, the goal is to write the document so well that the member of the press to whom I send it pops his or her byline on it and prints it, as is, in a newspaper, or reads part of it line-for-line on the radio. I have often written press releases and sent them to reporters along with review copies of a book, and soon thereafter have received a press clip from my clipping service featuring an article that printed my press release verbatim with a reporter's byline slapped on it instead of my name. I am sure that this doesn't exactly thrill America's leading journalism professors, but it happens all the time. In fact, it's the ultimate goal for you as a publicist, because it allows you to control and position information, primary and secondary.

Sample press release

Press releases come in all shapes and sizes. Here is a simple example:

FOR IMMEDIATE RELEASE:

For additional information, contact: Plug in your name here

Plug in your phone number and email address here

New PR primer offers back-to-basics rules that work in any medium

Plug in your CITY and release DATE here – While the rest of the world's media-seekers go mad blogging, tagging, and social networking, professional publicist David Carriere recommends asserting a little good-old common sense in his new book, *PUBLICITY: 7 Steps to Publicize Just About Anything*.

"People are concentrating on the medium so much these days, but in my opinion, it's the story and the content that you have to share that remains the primary connector," states Carriere. "New media social space offers amazing opportunities for clever flacks, but if you don't understand your own message or how, where, and when to communicate it, then it doesn't matter what medium you choose." Carriere believes that the fundamentals needed to generate publicity are timeless, and that to be successful, a good publicist needs to understand these principles before launching into new media spaces and opportunities.

In *PUBLICITY: 7 Steps to Publicize Just About Anything*, Carriere reveals all of the basics needed to mount a successful publicity campaign and shows the reader how to publicize just about anything from anywhere to anyone. Written for budding professional publicists as well as for ordinary individuals who want to generate press attention, **PUBLICITY** decodes what many newcomers consider the mystifying publicity process and explains how to move with ease from the early conceptual stage of a campaign and through to its execution and wrap-up.

In today's media-mad world, **PUBLICITY: *7 Steps to Publicize Just About Anything*** gives the reader license to be creative and the know-how and managerial skills needed to execute their vision. According to Carriere, "First comes the message, then comes the medium. Whether striving for success in print, online, or on the air, more often than not, it all boils down to first making human connections the old-fashioned way—by communicating."

PUBLICITY: 7 Steps to Publicize Just About Anything
By David Carriere
A Glitterati Book distributed by National Book Network
144 pages with blow-in "tip" card with adhesive backing
to hang on computer or wall
ISBN13: 978-0-9793384-7-2; Price: $20.00;
Publication Date: May 7, 2008
To learn more, visit: acarridedrive.org

Cover letter

I recently consulted with a client who had always assumed that different press releases were written for different target categories. For some reason, she thought that I would send a television producer a different press release than I would send a newspaper editor, but that is generally not the case. The bottom line is that your press release positions the same information for everyone equally, and that it's the one master document that serves as the cornerstone of the campaign, containing all of your key messages in a ready-to-be-published format. It is in the cover letter that you have an opportunity to personalize your pitch.

In the cover letter, the publicist customizes and tailors his or her message in order to appeal to each target individually. If I do not know the person to whom the letter is addressed, my tone is formal, courteous, and professional, but if I know the person, or if I have worked with them before, my cover letter and my tone reflect that and become much more personal. Whatever the case, I always try to hit the nail on the head by letting the recipient know up front exactly what I am looking for.

Many editors and producers receive so many pitches in the mail every day that they literally toss half of the stuff in the trash without even looking at it, the way you might recycle direct mail catalogs during the holidays, without so much as looking at them. If the recipient is actually taking a look at the content in your package and reading your pitch, then you must be up-front with them from the first sentence. People don't spend much time reading this stuff, so get to it, because you have only a moment to make a first impression and to keep your addressee's attention. To do this, start by combining your concentrated reduction with a description of what you seek, whether it be an on-air interview or editorial consideration. Tell your recipients what your product is or what your spokesperson has to offer and why they should consider it for a feature or a mention. End by offering additional information or materials and by letting them know how to contact you. Finally, state that you will soon follow up with them via a quick telephone call or e-mail, and don't forget to offer a sincere thank you at the end of the letter.

Press kit

A press kit is an assemblage of the various relevant publicity generating documents that are available to you. I consider press kits fluid and ever-evolving, because documents can be added and others omitted over time, but the centerpiece of any press kit will always be the press release. The press release is the first page any recipient should see when they open the kit.

Other pages in a press kit might include biographies, resumes, maps, or "facts and figures" sheets offering relevant lists, data, demographics, or other fact-based content—whatever documents you can pull together in order to fully tell your story. The kit must create a good impression and offer layers of information and credentials catered to the

Press kit checklist:

-Disc with photography or
  black-and-white headshot,
  if applicable

-Envelopes in
  corresponding size

-Stationery to reprint reviews,
  quotes, Q&A, and other
  miscellaneous content

-Postage

-Press kit folders

-Press release on letterhead

needs and mentality of the recipient. Sometimes, press kits even contain sample questions (with sample answers) for the press to ask a spokesperson during an interview. Such Q&A sheets are helpful to radio and television producers as well as to newspaper reporters who are on deadlines and tight for time. They also allow you the opportunity to suggest directions a producer or interviewer might want to consider taking. If you decide to include a Q&A sheet, keep in mind that it, at best, offers you some control, as you get to dictate the flow of conversation and guide the interview; at worst, it is simply ignored. Try to think of questions that make for good copy, and consider what the readers, viewers, and listeners would consider relevant. Another advantage to writing sample questions is that if the questions are eventually posed, then you and your spokesperson have already fully contemplated and prepared the best responses possible.

The intention behind putting together a press kit is to bundle information into a package that will get you more in-depth press. However, the days of elaborate press kits are over, and your kit should be kept simple for environmental reasons—including pages in a press kit just to beef it up is a waste of natural resources, recycled paper or not. The separate components that you choose to include in the kit should each tell their own story separately, and yet together tell the bigger, fuller story. In addition to generating publicity, an interesting press kit will also open up more potential retail venues, or might be the perfect tool to use to reach out to new partners and create new sales opportunities. For example, let's say you are a highly regarded fabric manufacturer in Manhattan and you have a press kit. The kit might be used not only to get you publicity but also to promote your business to new possible clients, such as interior designers, to whom you send the press materials along with a letter stating that you create customized curtains and textiles for home interiors.

Event and activity kits

Children's book publishers often create event and activity kits as ways for bookstores to stage in-store events that appeal to young audiences, or because such kits allow the stores to hold "authorless" events. These events are great grassroots opportunities for a book's publicist to generate a feature story or a photo opportunity in the local newspaper or online. You might hold a cooking class for kids to help launch a new cookbook, or create giveaway finger puppets for them while staging a puppet show to introduce characters that will soon be on a Saturday-morning television program.

Photography

As a publicist, you should consider making available photographs that showcase your product and/or your spokesperson. It has been my experience that if the press confirms that editorial coverage is in the works, and then you mention that you also have photography or "art" to share, the publication tends to use it, which means that your story expands and gets more page space.

When I wrote the initial draft of this book, it was still common to physically share thirty-five-millimeter images and/or black-and-white headshots with photography departments at magazines and newspapers. Nowadays, that practice is practically unheard of, because almost all art is submitted electronically. Product shots are common, as are headshots, and usage for such photography extends beyond press kits to newsletters, Web sites, signs in stores touting forthcoming appearances, window displays, etc. The only steadfast rule in sharing photography that has been designated for publicity purposes is that you always must provide the photographer's name, so that he or she receives a photo credit.

Sample video/disc compilation

If television segments are your aim, be aware that producers at the big national television programs often ask publicists for a tape containing a clip of other television segments on which the spokesperson has appeared. This tape serves as an audition, so if the spokesperson has appeared on any program before, for any reason, the producers want to see it.

B-roll

B-roll is existing footage that can easily be made available to the media as content for a story. Offering interesting b-roll can entice a producer to cover your story because it provides them with footage for free, and that footage enhances the story they want to create anyway. As long as the footage is relevant, it is usually appreciated by producers, at least for consideration. I once worked with Chad Pregracke, whose nonprofit organization, Living Lands & Waters, had a sponsor with a public-relations agency that shot some b-roll tape featuring empty barges on the Potomac River prior to an environmental trash cleanup that Chad and his team were about to conduct along the river's edge. Voilá! The footage contributed to a great visual when positioned against live footage a week later of barges full of trash that the volunteers plucked from the water. Such footage can always be used at another time in a number of ways, such as editing it into existing media interviews, or to make a looped tape (which automatically rewinds to play over and over again) that can be played in retail environments, at special events, in convention booths, or in store windows.

Media advisory

A media advisory (also known as a media alert) is not a press release as much as it is a special-event notice. It can be a stand-alone document or a companion to a press release, and/or it can be accompanied by a cover letter or e-mail. A media advisory is written to alert members of the media to all of the pertinent who, what, when, and where information regarding a scheduled press conference, ribbon-cutting ceremony, or other planned special event.

The publicist writing a media advisory should open the document with a brief paragraph, explaining what is going on and why, and should then offer the press all of the pertinent specific details.

I suggest that you literally write "What, Who, etc." on the left, followed by a colon, and give the pertinent details on the right, as follows:

> WHAT: Press Conference (state exactly what is
> going on.)

WHO: Mayor Smith (state who is involved, who will be in attendance, and/or who will be relaying the information.)

WHEN: Day, month, year, and time

WHERE: Location (offer cross streets and directions)

Then write a closing paragraph that offers any additional relevant (e.g., biographical) information, and close with your name and contact information. E-mail or mail the media advisory along with a personalized cover letter and other pertinent materials to the appropriate members of the press. In the days to come, it is worth following up with these targets by placing a quick phone call or e-mail to confirm that the information landed and to discover whether or not the reporter or media outlet will be attending. Then, the day before the event, call, e-mail, or fax again all of the press and the local newsrooms that have not confirmed attendance.

Wire services

For me, the expression "putting it out on the wire" conjures up thoughts of the telegraph. But the wire, a thoroughly modern method of communication, is a far cry from the beginnings of electronic information transfer. Today's wire services and news agencies will, for a fee, electronically distribute the press releases of various companies and organizations, in addition to other news alerts, directly to news organizations around the globe.

New technologies

Since I wrote the first draft of this book ten years ago, the biggest change in the process of generating publicity has to do with the proliferation of technology. The Internet has created and provided publicists with an entire new medium full of Web sites, blogs, social networking forums, and chat rooms to work with. At the same time, the emergence of Web technology has actually created a catch-22 scenario for many publicists, because as technology flourishes, it buries many trusted magazines, newspapers, and other venerable hard-copy print content providers as they come to be deemed obsolete, yet there is no denying that there are now more ways to reach people than ever before. It it not unusual for political candidates to announce their candidacy via Web sites, and word-of-mouth dialogue in chat rooms and on blogs has astonishing power and reach; it's a fast new world full of many options for immediate information dissemination. Thanks to technology, publicists have witnessed and even played a role in how and where the world exchanges information. Ironically, in the years ahead, the way that public relations professionals actually share and spread information will be overhauled as well.

E-mail blasts

The beauty of this information delivery vehicle (a grassroots wire service) is that sending out e-mails is free and immediate. The downside is that recipients are likely to forget or overlook them. If you want to cast a net with e-mail blasts, I suggest that you send out customized versions of your message to the various subgroups of people you know (family, school chums, hometown folks, clients, colleagues, and neighbors) so that you can cater your e-mail especially for them. I know an actress in Hollywood who sends brief e-mails to her extensive contact lists whenever she has news to share regarding a role in which she has been cast, and she always includes a link to her own Web site, urging the recipients to visit the site if they want to learn more.

Web sites

A Web site might very well be an important ingredient in your publicity efforts, but remember that the creation of a Web site is a two-step process, since it requires that you not only create the site itself but that you then find ways to drive traffic to that site. The task offers its own set of challenges, and you shouldn't allow them to pull you away from your primary objectives. Remember that your goal is to publicize your product, and to do that with a Web site, you also must aggressively publicize the site. I recently worked on a book project for a major publisher which, late in the publicity campaign, hired an agency to create a Web site, with the hope of reaching a younger demographic. All of a sudden, in addition to publicizing the book, my job was to generate attention for the Web site as well. This goes to show that these technology-oriented changes are abrupt and can be uncomfortable, but they are inevitable, and as a publicist you must be aware of and make use of them.

If you have no intention of creating a Web site, consider creating a presence for yourself or your product online in other ways. You can contribute editorial content to an existing site (which I will explore a bit more in the next chapter) or seek attention from blogs, for example. Another option is to set your product up for sale online (usually considered the job of the sales force rather than the publicist), or to create a profile for your spokesperson on a social networking site. Additionally, you might use existing audio and/or video files to create a podcast, and share that content online as well.

Blogs, bloggers, and citizen media

My mother recently asked me what a blog is, and my answer to her was that it is a diary posted online for the world to see. Little does she realize that the attention and influence usually attributed to traditional print media is in some cases quickly shifting to bloggers and their opinions.

Bloggers now have a huge and expanding influence online, and technology has introduced new ways to play the blogging game. This "citizen media" (as opposed to "mass media") gives the ordinary person a voice, allowing him or her to work collectively with others who share his or her opinions in order to draw attention to their views and ideas. Citizen media is just that, consisting of regular citizens who become empowered as their voices are heard. Together, they can influence public opinion to the extent that any enterprise that stirs their negative reviews or develops a bad reputation through them can easily be put out of business.

Social media release

The world of publicity and the methods through which the public relations industry shares information is changing quickly, and in the coming years, the typical ways publicists communicate information will rely less on old-fashioned press releases and more on the social media release (SMR). That said, the way you disseminate information as a publicist is changing and evolving, but the fundamentals and core principles of the publicity and planning process will not.

The SMR contains all sorts of content and formats this information in a new way, in layers like a Web site. For the publicist and the press alike, the benefits of SMRs are twofold. On one hand, they offer content and the opportunity to place and position a product for editors to cover or review, and on the other hand, they also allow the average reader the opportunity to post comments and to actually contribute to the content offered on the SMR itself.

A social media release positions key information and core news facts right up front, and it offers specific information, much like a press release, from copy to quotes to contact information. In addition, SMRs harness the power of technology and offer multimedia components that utilize the immediacy of the Internet. They might include video, interviews, photography, corporate logos, and links to other relevant Web sites.

As you can see, there are a number of routes you can take, and just like every other aspect of the publicity process, more often than not

LET TECHNOLOGY WORK FOR YOU

There are a couple of really great ways to let technology work for you and your campaign:

-Sign up for appropriate free industry e-mail newsletter blasts. As a book publicist, I subscribe to Publishers Lunch, and once a day I receive an e-mail full of industry news and happenings. There are hundreds and hundreds of others, from Crain's New York Business News Alert to DailyCandy. Have some fun searching for these online. Find the ones that appeal to you and keep you best informed, and sign up for them.

-Once you actually begin work on your campaign, sign up for Google Alerts and register your product, your spokesperson, and any other key words and phrases. Essentially, this ends up

being a free clip service that keeps you in the loop by sending you daily e-mails linking you to all online mentions of your product when you begin to score ink. It's a great way to track any coverage you end up generating, because the press doesn't always let you know. Otherwise, your alternative is to hire a professional clipping service, and though that's a great option, it's also costly.

the product and your budget will dictate the road you travel.

Bounce your press materials around

Writing is a process, so crafting your press materials, in whatever format, will inevitably take some time as you hone their content, draft by draft. I suggest that you avoid working in a vacuum by doing this alone. Bounce your content off of other people to get their opinions. You don't have to accept what your support system has to say, but it is easy to miss a simple mistake in your own writing that is very obvious to others. It is also important to hear your colleagues' takes on things. Their comments and suggestions are needed and welcome, and they might mean the difference between an ordinary document and an extraordinary one.

If writing is not your bailiwick, or if time constraints are working against you, and you know that you can't possibly be the one to write the press release or any of the other afore-mentioned options, then consider asking a colleague, friend, or family member to help you by writing a first draft for you. If that is not possible, consider hiring a journalist or technology major at a local college to help you write and create the initial documents. Once you have a solid first draft in your hands, edit and tweak the material as you see fit.

STEP 5: Map out the strategy

AT THIS POINT IN THE PROCESS, YOU MUST HAVE AN IDEA OF WHAT YOU WANT FROM ALL OF THIS. NOW, YOU SHOULD DEFINE YOUR REALISTIC GOALS AND BUDGET, AND MAP OUT A STRATEGY THAT WILL DELIVER YOU TO YOUR PREDETERMINED DESTINATION. What are your expectations? Where do you want to go? What do you want to get out of this? It's time to create an all-encompassing plan, and to commit to it. Be disciplined enough to take substantial steps toward reaching it every day.

Money makes the world go around

Even though mounting a publicity effort is not necessarily expensive, there are a number of costs that will inevitably come into play as well as many optional ones when you create a campaign. Costs may range from obtaining computers and software, to acquiring sample products for giveaway purposes, to shipping costs, to petty cash in the till for office supplies. The truth is that you don't need a lot of money to launch a campaign. However, the amount of money that you do have available for publicity purposes will affect the size and shape of your campaign and will ultimately dictate the amount of work that lies ahead. The budget will probably determine which ideas will actually become reality and which ideas were just parts of the brainstorming process. If money is not an object, then think big and consider casting the widest net possible. But if the bottom line is an issue, then get real, wrap your head around what's actually available in the checkbook, and understand your financial limitations. Focus your thoughts and your spending on the most important and achievable components of the campaign, and place those goals and targets first on your wish list.

Some line items on the ledger page offer more expensive options than others. For example, how do you intend on approaching people, and by what method of delivery? Will you be sending absolutely everything out electronically, or will you be using the United States Postal Service, or an overnight express service, or even a messenger to send out your press materials? The cost varies greatly according to which delivery method you choose. At the same time, consider the perception your choices will make. For example, does the method of delivery itself send a message and create a particular impression? Ultimately, your budget dictates all of the answers, and the ledger page will reveal whether your spokesperson flies coach, drives, or doesn't even leave home.

Starting a mailing list

Now that you have some plans in place and some press materials in the works, you must decide where they are going, when they are going, and how they're getting where they're going.

If you haven't done so already, compile a functional and very detailed, comprehensive database. Just as you must meticulously write and edit your press materials, you should also compile painstakingly accurate lists of potential press targets. But how do you know who to contact in the press when you really don't know anyone to begin with?

As always, get out your journal and begin by brainstorming, going with your gut. Start by listing the most obvious contacts available to you. This stream-of-consciousness approach will probably contribute more names to your database than you would initially expect. Creating a database is an ever-evolving effort, and just like the rest of the publicity process, it is a step-by-step trek.

When you start, you might not have correct contact names or proper mailing addresses for your targets, or you might be missing an e-mail address. Even if you don't have any specific address or contact information for your intended targets just yet, simply list the names or information that you do have as an entry, with missing pieces, and go back and fill in the blanks after you do more research. Just like writing press materials, start by just getting down what you already have to work with, then be a detective and fill in the missing pieces. Start by going through your notebook, your Rolodex, the phone book, Web sites, and the mastheads of magazines. Call the production offices at television programs and talk to the receptionist, and do whatever else you can think of to get the information you need.

In addition, make use of professional resources. Professional publicists purchase media directories from information services companies such as Bacon's Information/Cision media directories. These books list the name, title, phone number, and e-mail address of every employee at every magazine, newspaper, Web site, television program, and radio show in the country, organized regionally and nationally. Individual entries often include helpful little notes regarding each press person's ground rules with respect to solicitations from publicists. These directories cost hundreds of dollars to purchase, and they are invaluable if your budget has room for them. If your budget doesn't allow for them, don't worry. You should be able to find them at a good local library. Hunker down and fill in the missing pieces in the database, hole by hole.

Continue jotting down venues for contacts as they occur to you. These may include obvious Web sites, high school and college alumni magazines, your industry's trade journals, the local daily and weekly newspapers, and so on. As you will soon see, the skeleton of the list will quickly unfold and reveal itself. Approach your list from every which way. Think geographically and determine who the best targets are in the area where you live. Who are the targets in the town where your product is based? Who are the national A-list targets in all of the relevant media categories? As in all aspects of the campaign, think about the big categories while considering the small details.

Take your list to another level by thinking about the broad and specific industry categories from page 33 that you selected as related to your product. List names across those categories, and make category-specific lists. If you are promoting a high-end businessman's briefcase, then you should send your pitch to all of the obvious players in the "business" category of magazines, such as *Forbes, Fortune,* and *Business Week.* In addition, observe and record who specializes in writing about your product's category. For instance, your project might require that you help publicize a local nonprofit's theater production, and though you might not know who the local drama critics are, let me assure you that they exist in your region.

Finally, remember that many of the people in your life might know people who you'd be interested in contacting. They'll most likely be more than willing to share the connections they have, or they'll have great suggestions for you. Get on the horn or get online and work it the old-fashioned way by using connections. If people offer anything, then take them up on it.

What fields should you list in the database?
Whether you create various fields in a spreadsheet or list data in a word processing document, be consistent about how you record that data. Always confirm or gather any information you remain unsure about with a quick e-mail or phone call to the person or organization in question. Your database should include the target's salutation (Mr. or Ms.), first name, last name, title, company, address, city, state, zip, office phone, cellular phone, fax, e-mail address, and Web address. I suggest that you also include a "miscellaneous" column for odd nuggets of informa-

HELPFUL HINT

Never send a package generically to a studio or to a newspaper or magazine. Though there is a chance it will magically land in the right place, it will most likely get lost. Also, keep in mind that time flies, so as you build your database, remember to confirm information and to update lists before you use them. People switch jobs, businesses move, and information changes. It is important that you remain vigilant and update your lists as much as possible to keep them current.

Salutation:

First/Last:

Title:

Company:

Address:

City/State/ZIP:

Office phone:

Cellular phone:

E–Mail:

Web site:

MISC:

Code:

Follow–up

tion that you glean in conversations from this point forward, such as a birthdates, spouse's names, or the names of the towns where your targets spend their summers. Also, always include a "code" category so that you can distinguish magazines from newspapers and radio, etc. Finally, don't forget to include an additional column for follow-up notes.

Dig in a bit

Be honest with yourself. Should you look into your subject matter or a related area more than you have? Are there major media targets out there that you know exist but that you know you don't know anything about? If so, then you need to do your homework, because it will arm you with the ammunition that you need to make your pitch more targeted. Educate your-self, because if there is a big elephant out there that's not in your database, then it's your own fault.

Contacting the media by sector

The good news is that with the explosion of satellite and cable television and the Internet (on both computers and mobile devices), in addition to the stable of old-fashioned media outlets, there are certainly more opportunities to create publicity attention than ever before. As your campaign plans take shape, consider the sectors of the media that are available to you, and your strategy will begin to evolve. You'll realize which sector(s) of the media that you intend to approach, and which sector(s) you want to provide with publicity attention and why. As you build your list, your goal is to ensure that you have included the entire range of possibilities that exist in each major sector relevant to you.

Stagger in

It is usually best to send your product to just one person at any given publication or company at a time. You shouldn't send your business book to the managing editor, book editor, and travel editor at *ForbesLife* magazine all at the same time because you run the risk of enticing all three of them to cover the book. If they do, then you will probably have to jerk the placement from one or two of your contacts, alienating all of them. When I first started out doing publicity work, I remem-ber a photo editor at the *St. Louis Post-Dispatch* telling me over the phone that he thought it was ridiculous that I sent both him and the paper's book reviews editor a review copy of an expensive photography book. I knew he was right as he chastised me, and it was a great lesson because there was no need for me to be knocking on two doors at the same newspaper at the same time. My philosophy now is to stagger my knocks at the doors, and to approach only one target anywhere at any given time. Only when I am rejected by my first target am I free to approach another target at the same publication or program.

Magazines

Generally speaking, I recommend that before you reach out to folks at newspapers or television shows or elsewhere, you should first reach out to targets at magazines, because they have the longest lead times. It is common for the staff at the big national monthly magazines to work on issues coming out six months from now, so contact magazine editors as far in advance as possible.

The first group of magazines I tend to focus on when launching a product are the relevant trade publications. This niche group of magazines is published for and caters to the needs of specific industries, and it's just good business to start getting the word out in your own industry first. Whatever the industry, there is certainly a leading trade magazine that you should identify and approach very early on.

At the same time, I try to consider all of the consumer magazines pertinent to my product. These are all the big-name general-interest magazines you know and love. There are women's magazines (*Glamour*), and there are magazines for men (*Esquire*), and there are magazines created to appeal to special interests (*Food & Wine*), and general-interest magazines meant to appeal to everyone (*Vanity Fair*). Of course, all of these very big-time magazines have very long lead times.

Also, note that certain specialty publications might be appropriate for your publicity needs. These are the customized special-interest magazines produced to enhance a company's platform, so I recommend that you educate yourself and get to know the magazine world so that you can tailor your pitch to meet the needs of its editorial focus and readership. To familiarize yourself with the publications that you don't know, I suggest you visit the best nearby magazine stand, bookstore, or library and actually peruse copies of the magazines that surround you. Go online and see what else you can find. More than just knowing which names and addresses to add to your database, you should try to get to know the essences of all of these magazines, because editors get peeved when you waste their time trying to pitch them a story that is not a good match for their publication's editorial focus.

In the long run, if you really want to place your product in a magazine, remember that if at first you do not succeed, then try, try again. If you get shot down by one person, try another editor at the same magazine, or just try to work with another magazine. Both patience and tenacity are required—just keep trying. It can almost be amusing, as publicity attention does not always happen just when you want it to happen. Be prepared to systematically contact a lot of people in a lot of places now, but magazine placements will happen when they happen—not always on your time, but often on theirs.

National magazine targets are obviously not part of every

publicist's strategy, because they may not be necessary or relevant. Be aware of local and regional magazines that you might want to consider working with, or would have if you had only known their lead times! No magazine is too big or too small, and they are all equal as they stare at potential readers on the waiting-room table.

Television

From long-planned segments on a national television program to a "person on the street" interview for your city's six o'clock news, and from local independent-access stations to national network and cable programming with worldwide reach, the gamut of television publicity possibilities is immense.

As far as lead times go, as I said before, I consider magazines to be the first category to approach. National television is a close second. Television producers appreciate having a heads-up as far in advance as possible, because their field is highly competitive, and for them, time is literally and figuratively a commodity. Though a huge amount of television content is churned out every day, all day, on hundreds of channels nationwide, it is still best to pitch television producers as far in advance as possible. Each producer and program has its own set of deadlines; some are live and spontaneous, while some are planned long in advance. If your product is somehow tied to breaking news, then that type of coverage is obviously more instantaneous, compared to a human-interest story painstakingly produced and edited over a period of time. So, determine which scenario is best for your strategy, and find the right match, be it a talk show or the noon news or something on the

Food Network. Be creative, and think about possible fits as you work on your television target list.

Because some television news/entertainment formats, such as the morning shows, are live, you should know up front that there is an inherent danger when working with any kind of live television news program that they will bump you without warning for breaking news.

Television satellite tours

If your publicity campaign has a substantial budget, and you have an engaging spokesperson and an interesting story to tell, then you should consider conducting a television satellite tour. For this, your spokesperson reserves a block of time and the satellite tour company books a block of back-to-back interviews in different markets and on different news and entertainment programs. All of the interviews are scheduled together on one day, and all are conducted with the spokesperson sitting in one base studio as he or she is interviewed remotely by the various program hosts around the country. Though this can be a very effective way to reach different regions and markets, no bookings are assured, so it is a crapshoot as to which programs and markets will book your spokesperson. The good news for you as publicist is that it is the satellite tour company's responsibility to make the target list and to secure the bookings for you and your spokesperson. If you have never given this one-day approach any thought, take a look at your local television news or chat program and you will probably soon spot the show's anchor or host engaging a live interview with an author or actor in another city.

The reality is, satellite tours cost thousands of dollars, but if the bookings are substantial, it is an effective way to get a big bang for your buck instead of spending days or weeks and thousands of dollars on a tour, shuttling the spokesperson on and off airplanes and in and out of hotels. It's also an efficient use of time, if the spokesperson can't travel for long periods.

ACCESSIBILITY IS THE KEY

Do you want to glam up your database? Did you know that most politicians list their mailing addresses on their Web sites, and most celebrities can be contacted via their unions, agents, or other representatives?

Newspapers

There are a few daily newspapers in the United States, such as *USA Today*, the *Wall Street Journal*, and the *New York Times*, that offer ways to drive your message from coast to coast, but I typically view newspapers not so much as national placement opportunities, but more as very accessible local grassroots news vehicles. For the publicist, securing newspaper ink can be the perfect way to penetrate a particular market or many metropolitan markets.

I love working with newspapers because the regional "hometown" aspect of these publications instills trustworthiness and creates a very loyal readership. People are creatures of habit, so these newspapers have become cherished and ritualistic parts of many readers' daily routines. Therefore, if you want to generate publicity attention in a particular market, begin by adding the local daily newspaper with the largest circulation in that market to your database, and then work down the food chain, recording every other daily, weekly, and monthly paper as well. Almost every metropolitan market in the country has one newspaper that is the clear leader, as far as circulation and local prestige goes. Because of this, though you may end up having many other target names prepared and ready to go in your database, if time allows and if the circumstances lend themselves to it, you should consider approaching only the single most appropriate editor at that one newspaper first. Let that editor know that fact and that you want to do something special with him or her. If it doesn't work out, tiers of other major and secondary local newspapers, alternative weeklies, and tiny neighborhood newspapers alike also exist in most markets around the country.

Like magazines, newspapers employ a wide range of editors who are all drivers of their own truck in the convoy that is the newspaper. Each is captain of his or her own domain, and should generally be approached only with the particular pitch that will work for them. Many of these individuals must produce content daily, and on deadline, while others are weekly and/or tied to themes, so for the most part, their lead times are not as long as those of a monthly magazine or a television program lead time.

It is important to note that many larger newspapers create original special sections, Sunday supplements, or weekly magazines that have longer lead times than other parts of the newspaper. Some of these are four-color general-interest sections, and others are cyclical and often scheduled periodically, such as the "Education Life" section in the *New York Times*. My point is that there are plenty of newspaper editors who are not on breaking-news deadlines, so give them as much advance notice as possible.

If you are attempting to obtain publicity in your own backyard market, then start entering names into your database after taking a look at the local paper and jotting down the names of the local reporters that you like to read. Which ones would be the most receptive to receiving your content?

The first book I ever worked on (not as a publicist, but as an assistant in the photo department) was the tremendously successful *A Day in the Life of America: Photographed by 200 of the World's Leading Photojournalists on One Day, May 2, 1986*, edited by Rick Smolan and David Elliot Cohen. The book featured the work of many of the world's leading photojournalists, who fanned out across the United States all at once to various destinations in every state, where together they attempted to capture the essence of the nation as a whole on one spring day. The book generated huge national publicity attention and a number of cover stories in national magazines and newspapers from the top down, but what I found most impressive was how much local grassroots attention the publicity efforts generated from the bottom up. Much of this attention came in a number of waves. It first occurred in newspapers, when photographers arrived in a community to shoot for the book, and then the very same newspapers featured samplings of the local images that made the book (or didn't make the book) months later, when the finished publication was rolling hot of the press into readers' hands. Then, another wave of attention came at the end of the year in holiday wrap-ups, gift guides, and "the year that was" articles, etc. From then on, I have made sure to think about working big and working small, and always about working in layers.

All in all, it seems to me that though newspapers are currently my favorite way to penetrate a particular area, the newspaper category is currently the most vulnerable of all media. Newspapers are being forced to examine and redefine themselves in the evolving technological landscape, as the competition and opportunities that technology presents have forced them to drop sections and long-cherished content.

Newsletters

Old-fashioned hard-copy newsletters usually focus on one topic and offer a tactile reading pleasure that still appeals to many. There are more out there that are thriving—more than you might imagine. Do some homework online or consult a media directory to see which ones might be a good fit for your product.

Web sites

If you are going to use the Internet to position your product for others to cover, approaching potential online contacts is not much different than approaching editors or producers in any other sector of the media. If you want to share your content with online targets but you have no idea how to approach the process, begin by surfing the Web and figuring out which sites are a good match for you and your product. In addition to listing the sites you may be familiar with, type some keywords into a search engine to discover other sites that might also be appropriate. Peruse the "About Us" or "Contact Us" section of the site to discover the best staff member for you to get in touch with. Then, e-mail that person a note along with

HELPFUL HINT

Create an ongoing master running list in your journal or on your computer of each and every target to which you send anything, and when. Your e-mail out-box serves the same purpose for your online record keeping, but not regarding the press releases and other packages that you will be mailing or shipping. This task might seem ridiculous to you now as you read this, but I promise you that it will be an extremely important organizational component later on, when you are sending out dozens and dozens of pitches and trying to keep track of various details during the mailing process, and then again during the follow-up part of the project. You might think that you can remember who you sent what to and when, but believe me, it is extraordinarily easy to lose track and to believe you did some task that you didn't do; keeping a master list is a must.

your press release. In addition, other resources are available such as media directories that list and categorize online contacts. The bottom line is that even though we have new technologies to work with, we still have to make traditional person-to-person connections.

Radio

Radio is another example of a medium that continues to evolve, and whether through free terrestrial radio or subscription satellite radio, publicity opportunities abound. Radio, like newspapers, usually does not need a huge amount of lead time because of the 24-7 nature of the business. However, even though radio producers are constantly booking guests, you still should give the producer as much time as possible, because though they have time to fill, a lot of that time is already booked. Plus, you should build in time to cast a few waves of pitches, in case they become necessary. I suggest that you target your top pick first and attempt to arrange something special with that producer.

If you have breaking news, the magic of radio is that it can be immediate—and your spokesperson's voice might very well be on the air in a matter of seconds. Generally speaking, though, when approaching radio I tend to begin sending information to the producer at my first-choice station approximately two months to six weeks before the date that I am shooting to book. When contacting hosts and producers at radio stations, I often start very simple pitch letters or e-mails off with a mini headline (either in bold or all-capital letters so that it jumps out on the page right away) that states up front who is available for a live interview at the station. For example:

DAVID CARRIERE WILL BE AVAILABLE
IN DENVER, COLORADO
FOR INTERVIEWS ON MONDAY, MAY 15

I center that eye-popping statement on the top of the page, and then go on with the rest of my letter, full of who, what, when, and why information.

Sending your number-one target something two months in advance might seem like a long time, but good producers at good programs need as much time to work with as possible. It is to your advantage to have that time on your side as you help provide content for the program. Plus, if a book is involved, then it gives the interviewer some time to read the title. At the same time, it is prudent to work far in advance because if the station turns you down, or blows you off, then you still have enough time to approach your next-favorite target. I take it slow at first because local programs can be very competitive, and I want to tell my first-choice target in the market that my spokesperson is in or traveling to that no other local radio stations have been booked. (This is what you should do when you only have your spokesperson in a particular town for a certain amount of time and you want to book only the best first and then see what else you can do.) That said, different scenarios require different approaches, and if you're staging a press conference then you need to cast a wide net and contact everyone everywhere that you can, all at the same time.

Producers often prefer that guests be interviewed in the studio because the quality of the sound is better, but live and taped interviews can sometimes be conducted remotely. Your spokesperson doesn't necessarily have to be in the studio to be on the program; he or she might be at home in Seattle doing the interview, barefoot in his or her bathrobe. Again, in any interview conducted over the phone, the producer will typically request that the interviewee use his or her landline telephone rather than a cellular phone, for the sake of sound quality.

Radio interviews can be very nerve-racking, but they are not usually as intimidating as television interviews because the visual component is not part of the experience. No one can see, for example, that your spokesperson's knees are shaking on the radio. If your spokesperson is doing the interview in person, the studio often insulates from distractions. If he or she is being interviewed over the telephone, it is easy to get lost in the conversation once it gets going.

If you have to be aggressive but do not have much of a publicity budget, you can certainly reach out to many different radio stations in your area if your focus is regional. If your focus is national and your product is available around the country, consider lining up a block of interviews with as many drive-time morning shows or late-night talk shows in different time zones as you can. Occasionally, you will book an interview on one show thinking it will be heard in just that one market but the program is syndicated and airs in a number of other markets around the nation as well.

Radio offers publicists other unique and fun opportunities for additional mentions on the air, aside from interviews. For example, radio giveaways and contests can often easily be arranged with radio producers, who will mention a product on air in exchange for free samples of merchandise to actually give away to listeners. To arrange this type of event in tandem with an interview is ideal, and to do that, contact the producer or even the station or promotions manager at the radio station in the relevant city or region. If you do this, determine in advance what you absolutely require them to mention on the air and how often.

Public Service Announcement

If the product or endeavor you are attempting to publicize is for a good cause, then consider seeking free airtime by approaching radio and television stations with a public service announcement (PSA). If this interests you, I suggest that you first approach the program director or the public service director at the station, rather than a producer at a particular show. Stations are sometimes willing to give away unsold ad time as a PSA, which serves the station well because they generate goodwill in the community, and it serves you well in that it is one more cost-effective way for you to get the word out.

Assessing your mailing list

Though you should never stop brainstorming and adding the hottest names you can think of to your database, after a while there comes a time when your list will take some shape, and eventually there will be so many names that it will be tough to keep track of all of them. When that time comes, start thinking about dividing your mailing list into three different groups, categorizing individuals as A, B, and C targets. Look at the entire list and edit it down to the absolute A-list, with only the top dogs included. Then create a B-list and a C-list for everyone else. The B-list should contain the "probably" names, and the C-list is your "probably not" list. None of these names are set in stone at this point, so you can fiddle around with them a bit.

This isn't about playing games as much as it is about giving you a handle on what will otherwise at some point become unmanageable. Let's say you are representing a musician, and you want to issue a press release to accompany a mailing for a new CD. Your budget will allow you to approach one hundred targets, so you must determine which names on your list of 435 will be included on your newly created top–one hundred list. As you figure this out, you should consider a wide variety of publications and a broad swath of programs. Look for the very best picks from across the board on your list, and deem them appropriate for your A-list. Then, once you have that list, ask yourself who is on your top ten. Finally, if you knew that you could approach just one target, who would you want it to be? Whoever that top pick is determines the contact that you should approach first, if time allows. Know that you need to handle this individual a little differently than the others, as you are offering something special to this one target. Put together an exclusive, offering them the story before you offer it to their competition. When working with print mediums, this is often referred to as "serialization."

When I worked at HarperCollins Publishers in New York, I

handled a few pieces of the publicity efforts for a series of books created by famed *Peanuts* comic strip creator Charles Schulz. He was planning to visit Manhattan with his wife, not to promote the books but to attend a symphony composed in his honor, which was premiering at Carnegie Hall. Before he left his home in California, he stated that the trip was personal and that he wasn't interested in scheduling interviews with the press, but I asked him if he would be willing to squeeze in one interview for our cause when he was in New York. I told him that if he was willing to do that, then he should pick the one program that in the best of all worlds I would book him on. He agreed to do this and admitted that he was a big fan of television host Charlie Rose. If I recall correctly, he was very self-deprecating about his Al target and never assumed that this program would even invite him to appear. Of course, because Mr. Schulz (also known as Sparky) was literally loved around the world, booking him on the show wasn't hard at all; I think it literally took less than five minutes over the phone, without so much as mailing the producer a book or release. A few weeks later, Mr. Schulz and his wife were in town, and the three of us decided to walk on a crisp Friday afternoon from their hotel room to Charlie Rose's television studio, where we were warmly received and spent a wonderful hour or two as Sparky and Mr. Rose completed their interview.

A few years later, I hosted guests at my home in the Berkshires, and we went to the Norman Rockwell Museum, located nearby in the town of Stockbridge, where, unbeknownst to me, an exhibit had been mounted celebrating the work of the now-deceased Charles Schulz. In the middle of the room, serving as the centerpiece of the whole exhibit, a television monitor played a loop of the very Rose–Schulz interview that I had not only set up, but also witnessed firsthand from the sidelines. Until that point in my career, I had always considered magazines to be my favorite medium, because I felt that I got a lot of mileage out of magazine placements, since the results of my successful efforts often lasted for years in Laundromats. But at that moment, like never before, I realized that television programs also last, and can in some ways make an impact and be part of the time capsule that publicity can create. It gave me great pleasure to see the tape in the museum, because it was Mr. Schulz's own energy and intuition that got him the interview that became part of his own lasting legacy.

Timing is everything

Generating publicity is challenging under the best of circumstances, and often success comes down to timing and contacting the right person at the right time. Whether due to a little luck or careful planning, orchestration, and scheduling, serendipity will hopefully deliver your pitch to the right desk at the right time as destiny, luck, and chance all collide in your favor. Unfortunately, there is a flip side, and sometimes even the best-laid plans can be the victims of bad timing. For example, you might be in the midst of finalizing press materials and publicity plans to announce the opening of a new Italian restaurant, only to open your regional monthly magazine to find a huge article featuring all of the favorite local Italian restaurants. If that is the case, then your goal should be to determine how to set your restaurant apart from the others

HELPFUL HINT

If you are assembling a hardcopy mailing with a press release and personalized and customized cover letter, I suggest that you wait to seal each envelope until the very last step, especially if you are handling a large mailing. This ensures that if you by chance mistakenly put one target's letter in another recipient's labeled envelope, or make some mix-up with the pieces involved, then you can easily retrace your steps and correct the mistake rather than having to open all of the envelopes that you already sealed and redo all of the labels.

and how to proceed in order to score an entire feature article or a glowing review devoted solely to your eatery, never mind being part of a wrap-up article. Sometimes timing works for you, and sometimes it works against you, but it always seems to be for a reason and to shape your campaign.

STEP 6: Execute your plans and make them happen

L ET'S SAY THAT YOU HAVE TAKEN THE INITIATIVE AND SENT SOMETHING OUT, WHETHER IT'S ONE "A-LIST" PITCH ELECTRONICALLY OR A TWO HUNDRED–PIECE MAILING. IT IS NOW TIME TO CAPITALIZE ON ALL OF YOUR WORK TO DATE AND TO PULL IN THOSE NETS THAT YOU HAVE BEEN CASTING TO SEE IF YOU CAUGHT ANYTHING. Let's say your release is written, your database is done, and your envelopes are in the mail. Now it is actually time to move at full speed as you pick up the telephone and call or e-mail each and every one of your targets to explore if your pitch might be of interest to them on any level.

Follow-up

When it comes to following up, you must always be cognizant of the fact that there is a fine line between being persistent and being a pest. Frankly, the advent of e-mail has made the process of follow-up much easier for the publicist and the target alike because up until around the turn of the millennium you basically had to actually pick up the phone and call your target on the telephone. (Close your eyes and imagine my shivering voice uttering, "Graydon Carter, please," or "Hello. May I please speak with Larry King?") But now, hosts, producers, and editors don't pick up their phones as much as they used to, and you are not the only publicist seeking their time and energy, so it's better to follow up with them via e-mail because it's not as invasive as phoning. To me, it feels more like slipping a note in front of your contact, rather than ringing them and interrupting whatever they are doing. But the bottom line is that once a target has been forwarded a pitch, you are not going to know if they are interested in your work until you hear from them, and if they don't call or e-mail you (which many will never do unless they have to because they are just too busy) then you must call or e-mail them. I like to take it slow, and I tend to give the recipient enough time to receive the pitch, ignore it, then open it, read it, and let it sink in. But persistent I must be, so I note in my journal the date that the package went out on my running list, and if time is of the absolute essence, then I call a week later to the day. More often than not, though, I like to wait ten days to two weeks before I follow up.

When it comes to publicity in general, and follow-up efforts in particular, it is my opinion that a straightforward approach to language is often best. I suggest you introduce yourself and use my favorite follow-up line: "I am just touching base to explore if product X has arrived and if it might interest you on any level?" That's it—quick and to the point! If the recipient's answer is yes, that right then and there is the moment that the publicist lives for, the moment that you cross the line drawn in the sand and make a booking. This is when the conversations and the tasks will proceed to the next level and change on a dime, and the publicist transforms from the person who pleads to the person who performs. If, however, the target is not interested, then he or she will definitely tell you that, too, in which case you will dust yourself off and get on with it, calling or e-mailing the next person on the list.

If you actually have to use the telephone to follow up, then I have decided that it is best never to call reporters or producers for follow-up purposes on Mondays or Fridays. To me, those are the sacred days workers everywhere should be left alone to start the week up, and to wind the week down. On Tuesdays, Wednesdays, and Thursdays, the office is up and running, and people are more likely to actually be at work and willing to throw you a bone. When calling mid-week, I suggest you leave people alone at the very beginning of the day and at the very end of the day as well. I actually have the best luck reaching my media targets at their desks if I call them between 10:15 A.M. and 11:45 A.M. in the morning, and between 2:15 P.M. and 3:30 P.M. in the afternoon. I find that these hours are when they actually pick up the phone. The morning slot is great because aside from the noon-news folks at television stations, most targets with deadlines are not looking at the clock yet. Again, the beauty of e-mail is that you can contact people whenever you want, and they can respond to you when it is convenient for them to do so.

No matter when you make your calls, the sad reality of the situation is that throughout this follow-up process, you will probably be either ignored or rejected almost all of the time. Therefore, in order to proceed, you must be mentally prepared to handle rejection. You can't take a rejection the wrong way because this is business, and it's not personal. Be tough, and let it all roll off your back. During these vulnerable moments of rejection, I advise that you don't appear too needy. It can be scary to follow up, and it certainly might make a publicist feel nervous, self-conscious, and vulnerable, especially at first. You might call someone on a deadline who snaps at you under pressure, or you might contact someone in the morning who is angry that you are bothering them before they have their coffee. Along the way, some people will not be nice, but that usually doesn't have anything to do with you.

Whether you are e-mailing or telephoning, you only need to get one moment of your target's time in order to gauge their level of interest. That said, know that if your pitch to a member of the press is absolutely perfect on some editorial level, and if they want something from you regarding that pitch, then you better believe they will be picking up the telephone and calling you the first chance they get.

Whether they call you or you call them, once you get the thumbs-up from your press targets, you can explore what they need, and schedule an interview, book an appearance, or select photography to share with them. If the booking is for television, or if a photo shoot is involved, then a conversation about a date, place, and time should take place. Bring it up if they do not. If the interview is via the phone with a radio program in another market, then discuss the specifics with respect to the time-zone differences, and always inquire whether the interview is live or taped. Finally, note that if the interview is on radio or television, then you should always ask the producer up-front to make a tape of the interview for you. The same is true with newspaper editors from faraway markets. I am of the opinion that if the placement lands in an easily available national magazine or newspaper, you should leave those editors alone and pony up the coins needed at the newsstand, but know that most editors will offer you a tear-sheet featuring your product if asked.

Proceed with caution and believe it when you see it

Don't ever trust a promise that a story will appear in print or on the air until you actually see or hear it for yourself. There are many hands involved in the workload at a magazine or newspaper, and in the television and radio businesses, and since they are businesses, publishers and executive producers bump things at times for a variety of reasons. For example, a newspaper publisher who is having a big news day might decide to cut the review of your restaurant to make more page space for a feature article spilling over from the front page. Or, a magazine publisher might decide to cut the review of your art opening in order to accommodate the desires of a new advertiser. As I mentioned earlier, your spokesperson might be cut from a local morning show if some big, breaking news occurs. So, my golden rule is this: Never promise anyone anything until you have a copy of the publicity placement in your hands!

Confirmation letter or e-mail

As a safeguard in a profession with no safeguards, and because producers and editors are busy and on deadlines, and because people space out and forget stuff or get swept off in different directions, it is prudent to take a minute of your time to issue confirmation letters or e-mails to all involved to make sure everyone and everything is on track. Simply send concerned parties a quick computer-generated note if you have other materials that you also need to send along, otherwise send them an e-mail confirming the interview that you previously arranged, including a recap of all pertinent who, what, when, and where information. Such correspondence confirms that the booking was arranged, and reminds everyone of what is about to occur.

Here is a sample confirmation letter:

Dear (plug in producer's name here):

Just a quick note to confirm that David Carriere is scheduled to arrive at Harpo Studios (plug in street address here) in Chicago on (plug in day and date here) for a live interview with Ms. Winfrey in front of a live studio audience, etc.

Please feel free to contact me at 212-123-4567 or via e-mail at xyz@e-mail.com if I can provide you with additional information or materials.

Sincerely,

X

Publicist's name

You get the idea—just create a simple document recapping all of the pertinent prearranged details involved so that all players are on the same page. They can hold that page in their hands, which makes the arrangement real and which can help trigger a discussion if information is wrong or if something is no longer possible.

Executing a special event

Always remember, it's not an exclusive event if you do not exclude someone. I write that in jest, but the sad reality of the matter is that if you do your job really well, you might have to exclude people because you won't be able to invite as many people as you want! Without a doubt, an entire book could be written about putting together events of all kinds, but no matter what the special event is that your brainstorming efforts created, my first piece of advice is to start thinking about the numbers. Figure out how many people can be accommodated, work out the budget, and work the calendar to figure out how many days you have until the event. The size of an event party's guest list will be determined by the budget or by the capacity that the space can accommodate.

I have staged special events in all sorts of odd spaces, including in museums, on waterfront piers, in consulates, and in toy stores, and figuring out how many invitations to extend to the press can be tricky. Ask yourself: Does the press dictate the numbers, or do the numbers dictate how many press people can be accommodated? You can take a few different approaches to this. You can simply invite every important press person you can think of and then let all other numbers fall into place as they may after that. Or, you can come up with a number. A flat ten percent of all invitations will be reserved for the press, for example. Or, if there are other people or companies involved, then you should solicit both guest lists and press lists from each and every one of them. Then, cross out the redundancies on both lists to obtain an accurate base count. After you meld every guest list into one master database, then you will see how many seats remain that can be designated for publicity purposes.

Whatever the number of press may be, you should consider inviting various individuals from magazines, newspapers, television, radio, and online targets. Also invite any appropriate influencers such as local celebrities, politicians, and other "big shots." Again, I urge you to remember my "they need you as much as you need them" philosophy, so try to entice some glamorous people to attend, which will certainly add a little buzz to the room, and which offers all involved another photo opportunity. This might be easier said than done, of course, especially if you don't usually hang out with the mayor for Sunday brunch, but wherever you live, big city or small county, you must put together an event with panache.

Sample event invite

Each event is unique, so I can't exactly write your event invitation for you, but I can lay out a basic template that you can personalize and tweak as you see fit:

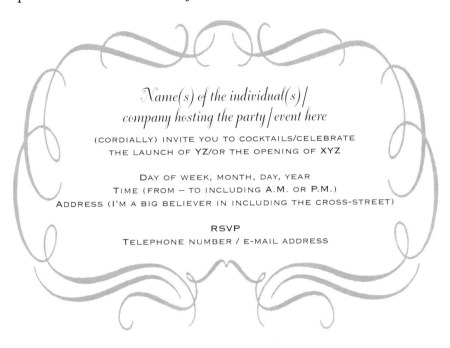

Name(s) of the individual(s)/ company hosting the party / event here

(CORDIALLY) INVITE YOU TO COCKTAILS/CELEBRATE
THE LAUNCH OF YZ/OR THE OPENING OF XYZ

DAY OF WEEK, MONTH, DAY, YEAR
TIME (FROM — TO INCLUDING A.M. OR P.M.)
ADDRESS (I'M A BIG BELIEVER IN INCLUDING THE CROSS-STREET)

RSVP
TELEPHONE NUMBER / E-MAIL ADDRESS

In my opinion, the less copy the better, as that keeps people focused on the crucial information. You can share this invite with potential guests as an e-mail, postcard, or formal invite on card stock in an envelope if the budget allows. However you distribute them, make sure that you include RSVP contact information. That said, know that people don't necessarily call or e-mail to RSVP, making exact attendance predictions difficult. Bring a print out of those who have RSVP'd with you to the event so you can control the guest list at the door if needed.

Be fastidious once the phone starts to ring

Let's assume that you have sent out your press materials in general, and that you have also just extended invitations to your upcoming event. You are e-mailing and using the telephone constantly, and everything is moving forward at full speed. Then, the phone rings, and the person on the other end requests an interview. You must listen carefully and write everything down in your journal during the course of the conversation, because if the phone keeps ringing, specific interview facts will begin to blur together.

In addition, pay careful attention to the dates the producer from the radio station is talking about, or to the month during which a magazine editor is interested in featuring your product, because you never want your one shot to be on the air or in the pages of a magazine before your product is actually available. If a member of the press is asking for a calendar date that doesn't work for you, pipe up immediately and steer them toward a date that will work. Don't ever wait to do this, because it will only get harder as time passes. For example, if a magazine editor agrees to feature a book that I am pitching and slots it for their January issue, but the book is not available in stores until March, I must convince that editor to wait until the March issue, because the January issue actually lands on the newsstands in December. There is nothing more frustrating for a magazine's readership and retail vendors than for the consumer to be enticed to buy something for the holidays that is not available until next year.

The old-fashioned tour

Putting together a media tour for an author, celebrity, or businessperson is a very labor-intensive task, and it is one that also falls on the publicist's shoulders. He or she is the person who will mastermind and juggle all of the coordinates involved with each city on the tour. Television bookings, newspaper and radio interviews, hotel arrangements, travel details and possibly media escorts must all be orchestrated for each city on the schedule. I definitely recommend that you hire a media escort in each city your spokesperson will be visiting, as that person provides a really important service as a local with a car who knows the area and who knows the locations of the nearby stations and publications. They should drive your spokesperson from one booking to another in their own backyard market. The bonus is that if you book an experienced author escort early enough, they will also surely have some suggestions for you regarding who to pitch for what, and may give you the names of some contacts. Also be aware that food stylists and wardrobe stylists can also provide great services if needed.

We have all heard a film star being interviewed on television, or a celebrated writer on the radio who mentioned that they were on the road conducting interviews on behalf of a project. Let's face it, if you're a movie star or a celebrated author, there is at least one publicist behind the scenes who is scheduling the itinerary and media bookings in cities from coast to coast, whereas for the average entrepreneur opening a restaurant in Holyoke, Massachusetts, there is not necessarily going to be a "tour." But in the same vein as my earlier recommendation to hijack the best of market research and to somehow appropriate the best of media training, I also suggest that you think of commandeering the best of what the tour offers. Just as a Hollywood publicist might break down the nation into regions for his or her client's campaign, you can break down your region into separate tour geographics. It's not always that you will be doing this stuff, as much as that you need to conceptually take from it what you can get, and allow what you take to propel you in a new direction. If working regionally, I suggest that you thoroughly examine and break down your own local market into four new markets. Consider the city just north of you a different market than the town to the south. Think of each geographic region as a completely separate tour destination, and set out to make publicity placements for your product or your spokesperson in each area. If you are representing a new eatery in Holyoke, then I suggest that in addition to publicizing your client in Holyoke proper, you also reach out to the press possibilities from Springfield, Massachusetts, to Hartford, Connecticut, to the south; from Northampton, Massachusetts, to Southern Vermont to the north; from Pittsfield, Massachusetts, to Albany, New York, to the west; and from Chicopee, Massachusetts, to Boston, to the east. Holyoke alone is one small city, but its location positions it within the reach of markets in four different states.

So, whether simply saturating your local market from top to bottom, or traveling from coast to coast, as the publicist, you must create a master tour document for your spokesperson that includes all relevant information and details and that lists everything in one place. These entries should be listed in calendar order by date and time. From flight times to hotel addresses to media bookings, *everything* is recorded on this master tour schedule.

Thursday, September 3, 2009

United flight # 123

Depart: Chicago (O'Hare) 9:00 A.M. (Central time)

Arrive: Atlanta 12:50 P.M. (Eastern time)

Escort: Mary Smith (phone number 123) will meet you at the gate in Atlanta and take you to your hotel, where you will have some time to eat and freshen up before your book signing.

Hotel name: The Bridge

Address: 123 South Street

Phone: 111 111 1111

Date:	Thursday , September 3, 2009
Time:	3:00 PM to 5:00 PM (EST)
Place:	Store name
	Street
	City, State, Zip
Contact:	Name of person at store
Phone:	Contact's number
E-mail:	Contact's e-mail

. . . and so on . . .

If your spokesperson is only in a particular town for one day, then your goal is to prearrange an interview on the most popular or appropriate television program for that day, as well as to book an interview on the hottest radio show. Ideally, the spokesperson has already conducted a feature interview with a local magazine writer in advance via phone, and/or an interview or review has been scheduled with one or more of the local newspapers. A presence should also have been made online in advance of the spokesperson's arrival, and a book signing, lecture appearance, or other special event should culminate the day. This event should be touted and promoted throughout the day in order to fuel attendance and sales.

For years, I have been arranging media tours for authors with best-selling potential, bouncing them around the United States and Canada on airplanes and attempting to book them on all the big shows in each market. I daresay that even though the majority of my efforts have been in North American markets, the process of generating publicity is the same worldwide, and my methods hold true in metropolitan markets everywhere, from Auckland to Sydney and from London to Toronto.

Budgeting a tour

Whether your spokesperson is traveling first class or coach, touring is obviously very expensive, and you must ask yourself how touring will affect your bottom line. If you are going to go through the tour process, you should have a handle on your expectations, because all of your efforts in addition to those of the spokesperson must translate into enough publicity to generate enough business to justify the expenses and time involved. Book all air travel and hotels in advance to get the best deals on flights and rooms, which not only saves you some money, but also lays down the bones of the tour. If you do not have an escort, then decide how you will handle getting the spokesperson to and from airports (this one item alone actually offers five or six options, ranging from prearranging a car and driver to taxis, shuttle vans, subways, and asking for a lift from a friend or colleague) and to and from the various interviews, appointments, and meals that you have arranged. Finally, whatever you do, I recommend that you build a ten-percent contingency rate into your budget's bottom line in case prices go up, or simply to handle any miscalculations.

A list of items your spokesperson should never forget when preparing to go on the road:
   -Cellular phone
   -Watch
   -Alarm clock that doesn't have to be plugged in
     (pay particular attention to time-zone differences)
   -Plenty of cash, including lots of dollar bills for
     tips at airports and hotels
   -Favorite outfits, professionally cleaned in advance
     and packed in the plastic in which they come
     back from the cleaners, so that wrinkling is kept
     to a minimum
   -Postage stamps, stationery, and hard copies of
     thank-you notes
   -Computer or other mode of giving the spokes-
     person daily access to e-mails

-Pen and notebook/journal
-Book to read
-Credit cards and frequent-flier
 memberships

If your spokesperson is traveling via airplane, then suggest that they pack everything that they need into one carry-on bag so that they will not have to deal with delays at the baggage claim or with the dreaded lost-bag situation.

What must be done along the way

One or two days prior to your spokesperson's appointment or interview, following up on the confirmation letter that you sent out weeks ago, you should now also give that appointment's contact person a quick call or shoot them a quick e-mail to touch base regarding the appointment. Confirm the time, the address, and other logistical details. Then, on the day of the appointment, it is imperative that the spokesperson arrive on time, even five or ten minutes early—but always on time at the very least, with no excuses.

PROPER BREATHING

The spokesperson might not be an experienced public speaker. If that is the case, remind him or her to inhale slowly through their nose and exhale slowly through their mouth, evenly, deeply, and calmly. He or she should do this over and over and over again, all the while working to consistently focus on nothing in this world except the very flow of their breath. This is a basic breath control technique that will help anyone to focus, assisting in staying calm as a person prepares for or lives through even the most stressful of interviews. Proper breathing takes a little practice, so urge the spokesperson to just sit still, relax, and focus on his or her breath on occasion, allowing all of the oxygen to help calm the body and focus the mind.

Do not overbook

It is absolutely crucial that a publicist book a day's various appointments with enough travel time built into the schedule between bookings to allow the spokesperson to get to and from appointments with time to spare. If you have your spokesperson booked for a thirty-minute radio interview on the outskirts of town at 10:30 A.M., and you want to add a television interview on the noon news that shoots downtown, then you should be straightforward and confer with the folks at the television station before you solidify the booking. Inquire how far the studio is from the radio station to make sure that you can build the necessary travel time for the spokesperson into the schedule.

After the interview

Whether the spokesperson is on tour doing a string of interviews, or whether the spokesperson is you, and you just conducted your one and only interview, I recommend that the interviewee always send a handwritten thank-you note (rather than writing an e-mail or placing a telephone call) to all of the interviewers, producers, escorts, and others who were hospitable to the interviewee along the way. Such a sincere gesture will certainly make a nice impression and will set the spokesperson apart from the rest of the pack. If the spokesperson is actually on the road traveling from city to city, then I really do recommend that he or she bring note cards (and stamps) and write such notes in daily installments on the road while the experiences are still fresh in his or her mind, rather than at the end of the tour when he or she returns home. At that point, the spokesperson will be jet-lagged, the memory of different people along the way will be fading quickly, and the task of having to write a huge pile of notes will be overwhelming. Very few people do this, because everyone is the producer's friend when they want an interview, but once they get what they want, people tend to disappear rather than express gratitude. Frankly, on a purely selfish level, it's also another opportunity to reinforce your spokesperson's and your product's good names in the minds of your publicity targets.

STEP 7: Allow your success to propel you forward

HOW MANY TIMES IN LIFE HAVE YOU HEARD THAT IT'S NOT ABOUT THE DESTINATION, BUT RATHER ABOUT THE JOURNEY? WITH RESPECT TO GENERATING PUBLICITY, IT'S ALL ABOUT DRIVING FORWARD TOWARD YOUR GOAL, WHICH MAY NOT BE ONE FINAL PLACE AS MUCH AS IT IS MOMENTUM AND WAVES OF ATTENTION. If destiny sprinkles some good fortune on your campaign, it is very satisfying if you can parlay that into two, three, four, or more waves of publicity, rather than attaining one swell all at once.

Whatever the case, it's all good, but note that because half of the job is getting the publicity, and the other half of the job is using that publicity, you must make sure to work with whatever publicity you get to propel your mission and goals forward, to fuel the sales machine, and to help the fiscal bottom line.

Tout and shout

Once you have actually scored some publicity, it is very important to start dangling that fact in front of colleagues, clients, the sales force, and the other players in your world. Once you have made your follow-up calls, you will have an understanding of which Web sites, magazines, and newspapers plan on reviewing or featuring your product, and which television and radio shows will be speaking with your spokesperson. This knowledge allows you to then begin to compile a thorough status report listing all of the periodicals and programs that have "confirmed" that they will be so much as mentioning your product, as well as a list of any "pending" placements with targets that have expressed sincere interest but have not yet confirmed a booking. Then, combine all of this information on one master (and hopefully growing) document and share it with everyone involved.

When you eventually possess articles and tapes that feature your product, send copies of them to the sales force as well, because it reinforces your product in their minds and hopefully gives them fodder for conversation when they are visiting their accounts and customers. In addition, alerting the sales force to publicity gives them the heads-up that potential customers are on the way, which might very well enhance orders. In fact, "publicity" is a word sales people like to hear very much because, aside from the massaging of the egos involved, selling is the whole point of generating publicity. Press can be good for self-esteem, but it is even better for business, and it doesn't do anyone any good if everyone on staff doesn't know about the publicity that is in the works. Distribute it, send e-mail alerts, make copies, and mount them on bulletin boards above the water fountain and in windows, make flyers and mail them, etc. Do whatever your gut tells you it's going to take to strut your stuff and share your hard work with one and all.

At some point down the road, consider including the best article that you generated in your press kit for those who need to seek new business opportunities, because such publicity placements become timeless archival pieces that often convey messages and impressions more objectively than your own press materials can. However, you don't necessarily want to include that same article in the press kit you compile to reach out to other editorial targets, because those editors might think, "Why on earth would I want to cover this if other publications have already beaten us to the story?" If they ask, you must certainly tell the press about other publicity, and if they show interest, you might even mention it along the line if things get serious, but don't mail new targets old publicity when you are initially courting them.

Clipping and taping services

When you actually make some sort of editorial placement, or arrange an on-air interview for your spokesperson, then know that come hell or high water, you need to get your hands on a copy of the issue of the magazine, or a copy of the televised interview, or a tape of the radio interview because that is the ammunition you need to inspire your sales force and others involved on your team. First, share the news about the placement, and then share the placement itself.

As I mentioned before, usually the editor will mail you a copy of the magazine or article from a newspaper, or the producer will mail you a copy of the program, but if that doesn't happen or isn't possible, then use a "clipping" service. These services employ people who read all of the daily, weekly, and monthly print publications in the nation, looking for mentions of their client's name, products, or spokespeople. The services then forward hard copies (as an original page or hardcover Xerox copy with a tab attached noting the publication's name and circulation) of all the articles or mentions that your product has received for the period of time that you have retained the service. For this, you will pay a monthly fee, and then an additional amount for each clip they procure. The nice part of this is that you get a hard copy of the actual article to hold in your hands. On the flip side, the results are not immediate, and there will be a lag time of several weeks between when the article was published and when the clip actually lands on your desk.

In addition, there are companies that tape all news programs and interview shows on regional and national television, so if your product was mentioned on a talk show in another city and you need to obtain a copy of the episode after it has aired, a copy is only a phone call away.

Whether or not you retain a clipping service, I again suggest that you take advantage of Google's free news alerts. These alerts essentially serve as a free electronic clipping service, and Google Alerts will send you a daily e-mail including links to every site that has mentioned the name or words that you registered when you signed up for the service.

If you've got it, flaunt it
When the time comes, go through all of the articles and all of the mentions and all of the miscellaneous press that you generated, and select the best quotes. For your press kit, compile

a best-of-the-best page boasting quote after quote, listing their sources and the dates they aired or were published.

If a large quantity of publicity attention is generated, bind it in book form

If you accumulate a substantial amount of publicity attention, an impressive way to share the ink you created (whether you are sharing it with colleagues or the sales force is sharing it with accounts) is to make a booklet with copies of all of your print placements "to date," presented together as a body of work, all in one place. A ribbed spine binder or even a simple three-ring binder will work. Xerox the articles, consistently and neatly, and on the bottom of the page (bottom center or bottom right only, rather than on the left side where the binding will be) type the name of the publication, the date it appeared in print, and the magazine or newspaper's circulation number. In general, organize the pages in order of publication, but if any really impressive or high-profile publications are involved, then you may want to position those placements as the first few pages, and then proceed in date order.

Publicity's relationship to sales

Neither the immediate impact of a publicity campaign nor the long-term consequences of its success are actually quantifiable. At the same time, sales results end up on a ledger page, and at the end of the day, publicity exists to create the attention that translates to business and creates sales. Though publicity is not quantifiable, sales numbers will act as your barometer.

If there is a sales team, and if you have the luxury of solely focusing on publicity and haven't had much communication with your colleagues, then I urge you to visit the sales force's world as early as possible in your campaign. You should know how the sales force is positioning the product. Find out if they need anything from you in the future or if you can enhance their efforts in any way with what you have already accomplished or with the press materials that you have created and have on hand. Offer the sales force copies of press releases, biographies, photos, or anything else that is available for them to share with their accounts. Sometimes these accounts, such as independent stores and chains, can use the press materials for their own newsletters, online content, and local media contacts. Maybe this publicity will be the impetus needed to get a chain of airport stores to finally buy your product, or maybe the publicity will help secure valuable store space for display purposes in other retail environments.

As far as the future goes, what are the expectations of the sales force? The way the sales force is positioning your product will certainly be of interest to you. Is there a category upon which you can now focus to generate some attention that would aid the sales force in doing its job in the future? As a publicist, pay attention to where the sales force is putting its energy and try to create a wave of publicity that might help them. Generating publicity takes time, so quick fixes are hard to accomplish, but the publicist should be fluid enough to go with what sales is telling them or asking of them.

One thing you should find out is how the sales department alerts its sales force around the region or the country regarding upcoming or recent publicity, so that you can contribute to that effort. I know of one book distributor who organized what they called a "white box mailing" to be mailed to their sales force every month or so. If one had a hard copy of a publicity report to share with them, or a copy of a magazine or newspaper article that might be of interest to them, or a signed copy of a book especially for them, one could give the sales assistant these promotional items. The assistant would then mail these materials to sales representatives across the country in these "white boxes." I loved this, because not only was everyone figuratively on the same page, but they were also literally holding the same page in their hands. Whether or not you have a little white box for relaying information, you have both "confirmed" and "pending" ammunition, and other major information regarding the publicity campaign, that you can provide for the sales force on a regular basis. Share whatever you have that will help them do their job.

There is a temporal element to disseminating publicity information as well, so make sure you provide your sales force with the publicity arsenal they need in a timely manner. There are two time periods in the sales process during which publicity can help deliver sales results that make an impact on the product's bottom line. These time periods are known as the "sell-in" and the "sell-through."

The sell-in
This section doesn't apply to every reader of this book, because every publicity effort is different. Some publicity projects do not have a sales component, but if it is your responsibility to publicize a mass-produced product such as a music album, a

toy, a movie DVD, a book, or even your own line of handmade clothing, then you have a major role to play in assisting sales during two different phases.

First comes the sell-in, which is the period in the sales process when the sales force rolls out and dangles the product in front of various retail outlets, attempting to entice them to order the product and offer it for sale on their shelves. This is the time when the publicist supports the efforts of the sales force by informing them of the product's publicity potential and by securing advance publicity regarding the product in trade publications so the sales team can in turn inform the retailer that the product will be receiving the attention that it deserves. Let's just say that the publicist and the publicity process can help build a bridge to an optimistic future for the sales force during the sell-in process. Of course, keeping the sales force up to date and informed of your publicity efforts is your responsibility as publicist. Just as publicists must work in advance, so does the sales force, so they need as much information to work with as early as is possible. What good is forthcoming publicity if no one knows about it?

The sell-through

Once a product is sold into a store and is sitting on the shelf for sale, then obviously it has been sold in, and that's a crucial accomplishment. But now it must sell through to the customer, and that is paramount if anyone expects to make any money! The sell-through is the second half of the sales process, during which the product actually moves from the store's inventory through the checkout counter and becomes the consumer's new possession. This is the quantifiable sales piece of the equation, which becomes part of the ledger page, and it is publicity's goal to generate the attention that informs the consumer about the product and that somehow triggers them to drive to the store. Otherwise, if it doesn't sell through, it is returned, and everyone loses when merchandise is returned. The cruel irony of the whole process, though, is that even if you score mounds of attention for your product, that attention doesn't necessarily translate to sales. It probably will, but again, when it comes to publicity, there are no guarantees.

Finally, publicists also often work directly with the sales department and sales representatives to determine which store(s) in a certain territory they should approach to arrange an appearance, autograph-signing, or other special event. At times, you might even be able to arrange a series of events with one particular account, such as sending a chef on a tour through a few specialty cookware stores in a regional chain. Obviously, such account-specific promotions require that the publicist not only help schedule and orchestrate each particular event, but also that he or she line up press about the event beforehand, finding various ways to inform and attract potential attendees in advance of the appearance. The publicist must then again arrange press coverage to cover the event itself.

WARNING
Publicity can be like an addictive drug!
Through the years, I have worked on literally hundreds of campaigns and have had the pleasure of working with a wide variety of clients who possess a myriad of personalities.

Sometimes, the minute a campaign begins, clients suddenly become hooked on publicity like it's an all-powerful, addictive drug. Sometimes, people lose perspective once they get a taste of favorable publicity, and their egos and self-esteem become involved, leading to cravings for more and more publicity. The more publicity you generate for them, the more they like it; and the more important they feel, the more they expect to receive publicity—it becomes a vicious cycle. Even if those involved don't become raging lunatics, developing and executing a publicity campaign can be more stressful than it has to be if you spend too much energy focusing on the hopes, expectations, and demands of your client or your spokesperson. On the one hand, you should be supportive, but on the other hand, you should avoid taking on the role of enabler or babysitter. I advise you to focus on the work that I have outlined in this book, envisioning the realistic opportunities in front of you rather than indulging the magazine-cover fantasies of others.

Integrity must be an ingredient in the mix

When I wrote the first draft of this book, I included a paragraph about the necessity of always being honest and always having integrity through the entire publicity process. I emphasized that one must maintain only the highest professional standards when working to generate publicity, but I kept cutting the section out in various drafts, because I worried I was being too pious. But I've decided that I have to be up-front and talk about this very important matter because it is very easy to be enthusiastic about your product and to all of a sudden find yourself exaggerating facts or embellishing numbers as you attempt to entice a reporter to cover your product, or as you are in the midst of an interview. You must never, ever do that. Know this now, before you even begin to write your press materials, and before you begin to contact the press: Facts and sales figures are quantifiable, but your reputation is not. Ultimately, your reputation is all you have, and it is what is on the line. Plus, the reporter on the other end is giving you their trust, and their reputation is also on the line. People take their own reputations seriously, so don't ever jerk them around. Be honest throughout the publicity process, and make sure everyone on your team is truthful as well, because exaggeration, gossip, and outright lies will do nothing but come back around again and bite you.

Perseverance must be an ingredient in the mix

As I wrote in the beginning of this book, focus on the destination and set specific goals in order to travel the journey with clarity, imagination, and vision. If you do, your persistence will pay off handsomely. Move slowly, step by step, and cast a wide net, which will statistically increase your chances for success. Always follow up on your initial effort. Your media target may pass on your pitch this time around, but that doesn't mean that your message wasn't heard or that you didn't make an impression that will later pay off.

In conclusion

You have a million excuses, and probably quite a few fears, but the bottom line is that if you are going to truly work to generate publicity attention, then you have to commit to your gut instincts. Start by doing something, however small, each and every day to take you in the right direction. At the very least, you'll get to know yourself in a new way while on the journey, and the publicity campaign will help you examine the place your product occupies in the world in a new way. I've given you the keys, now you can get behind the wheel and go on your own publicity journey.

RESOURCES

Communication/Media training: The Lisa Ekus Group, LLC
http://www.lisaekus.com/media-overview.asp
Timothy Cage Communication Training, LLC
email: Tccom@aol.com

Free electronic alerts: Google
http://www.google.com

Media monitoring services: Cision (formerly "Bacons")
http://us.cision.com

Press clipping services: BurrellesLuce
http://www.burrellesluce.com

Publication to advertise interview availability:
Radio-TV Interview Report
http://www.freepublicity.com/rtir

Wire services: Business Wire
http://home.businesswire.com

I hope that the advice in this book serves you
well. For additional information, please visit
www.acarridedrive.org
or
www.davidcarriere.org

ACKNOWLEDGMENTS

I am whom I am as a publicist because of the following teachers and colleagues, past and present, and I offer my sincere gratitude to each and every one of these individuals for everything they have taught me:

Marilyn Allen

Lisa Alther

Larry Ashmead

Lyn Austin

Jennifer Barry

Signe Bergstrom

Lisa Berkowitz

Nan Bernstein

Carole Bidnick

Fran Black

Cathy Blaser

Anne Bogart

Nicholas Callaway

Woodfin Camp

Rose Carrano

Jennie Cernosia

Martha Clarke

Nick Clary

Catherine Clucas

David Elliot Cohen

Jenny Collins

Fleur Cowles

Debbie Donnelly-Robinson

Lisa Ekus-Saffer

John Engels

Marcy Engelman

Jennifer Erwitt

Ken Geist

Mary Ann Gilderbloom

Jennifer Grace

Maria Griffin
Marta Hallett
Josh Haner
Ellen & Andrew Hathaway
Caroline Herter
Kathryn Howard
Maria Hjelm
Molly Ioannou
Amy Janello
Jack Jensen
Lois Jensen
Courtney Johnson
Jessica Jonap
Leslie Jonath
Carey Kaplan
Maureen Anne Teresa Kelly
Buff Lindau
Paula Litzky
Tim Lovett
Devereux McClean
Scott McClean
Nion McEvoy
Sarah McFall-Bailey
Clio McNicholl
Cathryn Michon
Jody Milano
Isolde Motley
Gayatri Mullapudi
Bill Neuert

John Owen
Paul Palmer-Edwards
Gina Privitere
Cathy Quealy
David Rakoff
Miki Raver
Patti Richards
Jean Salvadore
Molly Schaeffer
Stephanie Sherman
Jill Siegel
Rick Smolan
Stephen Sorrentino
Adrienne Sparks
Lara Starr
Oliver Stone
Elizabeth Sullivan
Lena Tabori
Kelley Vickery
Diane Wondisford
Zoë